Commuter Students: Enhancing Their Educational Experiences

Sylvia S. Stewart, *Editor*

NEW DIRECTIONS FOR STUDENT SERVICES

URSULA DELWORTH and GARY R. HANSON, *Editors-in-Chief*

Number 24, December 1983

Paperback sourcebooks in
The Jossey-Bass Higher Education Series

Jossey-Bass Inc., Publishers
San Francisco • Washington • London

Sylvia S. Stewart (Ed.).
Commuter Students: Enhancing Their Educational Experiences.
New Directions for Student Services, no. 24.
San Francisco: Jossey-Bass, 1983.

New Directions for Student Services Series
Ursula Delworth and Gary R. Hanson, *Editors-in-Chief*

New Directions for Student Services (publication number USPS
449-070) is published quarterly by Jossey-Bass Inc., Publishers.
Second-class postage rates paid at San Francisco, California,
and at additional mailing offices.

Correspondence:
Subscriptions, single-issue orders, change of address notices,
undelivered copies, and other correspondence should be sent to
New Directions Subscriptions, Jossey-Bass Inc., Publishers,
433 California Street, San Francisco, California 94104.

Editorial correspondence should be sent to the Editors-in-Chief,
Ursula Delworth, University Counseling Service, Iowa
Memorial Union, University of Iowa, Iowa City, Iowa 52242
or Gary R. Hanson, Office of the Dean of Students,
Student Services Building, Room 101, University of Texas
at Austin, Austin, Texas 78712.

Library of Congress Catalogue Card Number LC 82-84206

International Standard Serial Number ISSN 0164-7970

International Standard Book Number ISBN 87589-972-2

Cover art by Willi Baum

Manufactured in the United States of America

Ordering Information

The paperback sourcebooks listed below are published quarterly and can be ordered either by subscription or single-copy.

Subscriptions cost $35.00 per year for institutions, agencies, and libraries. Individuals can subscribe at the special rate of $21.00 per year *if payment is by personal check.* (Note that the full rate of $35.00 applies if payment is by institutional check, even if the subscription is designated for an individual.) Standing orders are accepted. Subscriptions normally begin with the first of the four sourcebooks in the current publication year of the series. When ordering, please indicate if you prefer your subscription to begin with the first issue of the *coming* year.

Single copies are available at $7.95 when payment accompanies order, and *all single-copy orders under $25.00 must include payment.* (California, New Jersey, New York, and Washington, D.C., residents please include appropriate sales tax.) For billed orders, cost per copy is $7.95 plus postage and handling. (Prices subject to change without notice.)

Bulk orders (ten or more copies) of any individual sourcebook are available at the following discounted prices: 10–49 copies, $7.15 each; 50–100 copies, $6.35 each; over 100 copies, *inquire.* Sales tax and postage and handling charges apply as for single copy orders.

To ensure correct and prompt delivery, all orders must give either the *name of an individual* or an *official purchase order number.* Please submit your order as follows:

Subscriptions: specify series and year subscription is to begin.
Single Copies: specify sourcebook code (such as, SS8) and first two words of title.

Mail orders for United States and Possessions, Latin America, Canada, Japan, Australia, and New Zealand to:
Jossey-Bass Inc., Publishers
433 California Street
San Francisco, California 94104

Mail orders for all other parts of the world to:
Jossey-Bass Limited
28 Banner Street
London EC1Y 8QE

New Directions for Student Services Series
Ursula Delworth and Gary R. Hanson, *Editors-in-Chief*

Contents

Editor's Notes

The major goal of this sourcebook is to assist the practitioner in changing the campus environment so that commuter students' learning opportunities are enhanced. Improving the programs and services for commuters therefore, may help them to persist in school. But the development of examples of good practice in student services/development programs for commuter student populations has been slowed by six factors described below.

First of all, the history and tradition of higher education is residential. In many institutions, this image is perpetuated by the memories and experiences of faculty, staff, alumni, and others, long after a shift to a predominantly commuter student population has taken place. Second, commuter students constitute a heterogeneous group. The definition of the commuter student population is multifaceted and understanding by institutional personnel of the subgroups, as defined through research, has been quite limited to date. Third, much of the present activity in the student personnel profession has centered on debating not only how to define commuter students but also whether such students should be treated as a campus subgroup that is handled by general student services or if a separate functional area or office should act as an advocate and provide services and programs specifically for commuter students.

The fourth factor that has slowed development of good services for commuters is that much of the awareness and description of the commuter student phenomenon began at a time when most institutions were faced with shrinking resources. Adding a new group to the long list of those who already needed administrative attention has been met with resistance in many cases. Fifth, in those institutions where action for commuters was implemented, the staff assigned to such programs have been, for the most part, located in relatively low levels of the organizational hierarchy. Therefore, they have been less likely to affect overall institutional change. Finally, the general challenge of accommodating commuter students has been coupled with a lack of interest on the part of these students. Low group identity and limited involvement with the institution on the part of commuters has led to the absence of the development of commuter students as a strong constituency group at an institution.

This sourcebook focuses on recommendations for overcoming these obstacles to serving commuter students. Chapter One by Sylvia Stewart and Penny Rue describes the variables that define the commuter student population and outlines their strong presence in all segments of higher education. In Chapter Two, Rosalind Andreas suggests that conducting an institutional self-study to examine an individual institution's response to its commuter student population is a must for understanding the diversity of a campus' students. More specifically, the findings of an in-depth study of how twenty campuses provide services to commuter students are presented by Penny Rue and Jeanne Ludt in Chapter Three. Staffing, funding, and examples of services, programs, research, and advocacy are also outlined there.

Barbara Jacoby examines the dependent commuter — the student who lives at home with his or her parents — in Chapter Four. She highlights recommendations for involving parents in the higher education environment. Chapter Five by Lee Knefelkamp and Sylvia Stewart is a discussion of problems and opportunities for applying student development theories to commuter students as a separate group. They chart needed institutional changes as well as challenges for student affairs practitioners in the improvement of services for commuters. Finally, in Chapter Six Sharon Taylor and Sylvia Stewart list more than one hundred examples of good practice that can be implemented to enhance the educational experience of commuter students.

Sylvia S. Stewart
Editor

Sylvia S. Stewart is director of commuter affairs and the National Clearinghouse for Commuter Programs, University of Maryland, College Park.

The changing demographics of higher education require a comprehensive definition of commuter students.

Commuter Students: Definition and Distribution

Sylvia S. Stewart
Penny Rue

The definition of the commuter student population is not only complex but is also hindered by the absence of comprehensive data that describe participants in higher education in general. Much of the available national commentary on commuter student characteristics unfortunately is limited to a discussion of full-time students (Chickering, 1974; Astin, 1975, 1980). Recent writing and discussion by members of the student personnel profession has focused on the changing demographics of higher education and, more specifically, on the adult learner (Brodzinski, 1980). Both of these directions leave the definition of the commuter student incomplete.

However, in writing for the *NASPA Forum,* we recently offered the following discussion that begins to define the commuter student comprehensively. "As student affairs staff members in higher education working with, for, and on behalf of commuter students, we are often in a position to bring the needs of these students to the attention of colleagues in various positions. Commuters currently represent approximately 80 percent of the overall undergraduate population in

S. S. Stewart (Ed.). *Commuter Students: Enhancing Their Educational Experience.* New Directions for Student Services, no. 24. San Francisco: Jossey-Bass, December 1983.

higher education. In some recent conversations we found that we were having difficulty making ourselves understood as we talked about commuters. As we tried to clarify our meaning, we realized we had inappropriately assumed a shared understanding of what was meant by the term *commuter...* " (Rue and Stewart, 1982, p. 8). Most commuter affairs specialists use *commuter* to convey the broadest possible meaning: those students who do not live in university-owned housing on campus. However, commuters are made up of a number of different subgroups, and not all subgroups are represented on each campus. In addition, different subgroups are distinguished by characteristics that also define the kind of services they require. Our intention here is to outline the various demographic dimensions along which commuter students vary so that the profession can reach a shared understanding of who the commuter student is.

Some common perceptions and myths about commuters are worth examining first. In most cases, these perceptions reflect outdated or provincial perspectives. One of the most common misperceptions is to think of all commuters as "townies" or day students. This term refers to the traditional-aged college student, aged 18-to-23, who lives at home with his or her parents. In the past, this student may have been given provisional or conditional admission status, and hence the "townie" label took on a derogatory overtone. Another unfortunate stereotype of the student who lives at home is of someone tied to mother's apronstrings, who is unable to begin the appropriate college task of developing autonomy. In contrast, administrators who remember the difficult times of the 1960s protest era may persist in seeing commuters as troublemakers who fought for the right to live off-campus. Commuters may be perceived as disinterested in the life of the college or unable to adapt to group living. And administrators may not be able to shake themselves of the notion that, if students really cared about a campus, they would live on it.

A different, more recent misconception is that commuters are mainly nontraditional students. It is true that most nontraditional students (defined as being over 25 years old) are in fact commuters. However, it is not true that most commuters are nontraditional, although that may be the case on some campuses. In any case, nontraditional students are those the typical student affairs professional has been least prepared to assist. Staff members thus may fail to reach out to commuter students because they feel that commuters are beyond their reach. A similar problem exists when staff members view commuters as primarily evening or part-time students. These students by definition have other commitments and roles outside of school, and they may be perceived as not interested in or in need of the student services provided by their college or university. As a group, such students are easy to neglect because they usually do not arrive on campus until most of the student services staff have gone home.

Each of the above myths represents a highly stereotypical view of a particular subgroup of the commuter population. Of course, these subgroups often overlap. To clarify the situation, we have identified three variables that are the most important or useful in distinguishing the population. Since where the commuter lives may have the most bearing on how he or she will interact with the university, the first variable is that of dependence versus independence. Students defined as dependent live at home with parents or a close relative who assumes parental responsibilities. Independent students live on their own; they may share an apartment or house, have a place to themselves, or even live in fraternity or sorority housing. Another important demographic aspect of the commuter student is whether he or she is traditional or nontraditional. As suggested above, a nontraditional undergraduate student is one who falls outside of the typical student-age group. We define *nontraditional* as referring to those who are 25 or older. These students often have returned to school after a break in their education. They may have a spouse or children. The last variable that has a significant impact on the understanding of commuters and their needs is whether they are part- or full-time students. Although this is defined differently in terms of the number of credit hours taken at different schools, it is a reflection of what else may be going on in a student's life.

The interactions between these three variables yield eight distinctly different types of undergraduate students: (1) dependent, traditional, full-time; (2) dependent, nontraditional, full-time; (3) dependent, nontraditional, part-time; (4) dependent, traditional, part-time; (5) independent, traditional, full-time; (6) independent, nontraditional, full-time; (7) independent, nontraditional, part-time; (8) independent, traditional, part-time (see Figure 1).

Almost all resident students fall into the category of independent, traditional, and full-time. To clarify the different types of commuter students, the characteristics of someone who might fit each category are described below:

1. A new freshman who lives at home because of financial constraints, or because on-campus housing is limited
2. A recently divorced woman with children who has returned to her parents' home while in school
3. A veteran who lives at home and works

Figure 1. Status of All Undergraduate Students in Higher Education by Three Variables

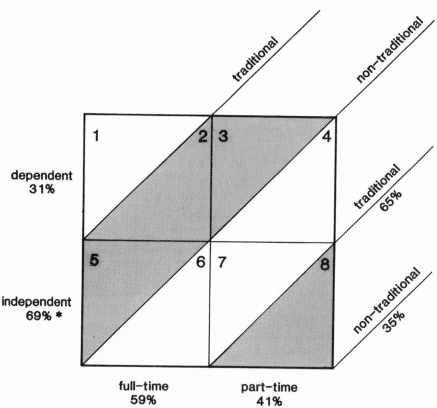

full–time 59% part–time 41%

*Includes 21 percent in university-owned housing, 36 percent in own place of residence, and 12 percent in other off-campus arrangements.

Sources: Astin, 1980; Carnegie Council on Policy Studies in Higher Education, 1981; National Center for Education Statistics, 1981; U.S. Bureau of the Census, 1980.

4. A 19-year old who lives at home and works
5. An international student who attends school full-time supported by her government
6. An older student who has returned to school on a full-time basis after work
7. An adult student with a full-time job and family, who is taking one course a semester for personal development
8. A student living in her own apartment, who works to support herself and goes to school part-time.

Of course, individual students may switch from full-time to part-time and dependent to independent statuses at multiple points in their academic careers, which further complicates efforts to understand the impact of the education they receive. In addition, another distinguishing variable in the definition of different types of commuter students on a campus is the institutional location—whether it is urban, suburban, or rural. This factor might provide insight into special institutional missions or student needs.

In general, how are these student variables distributed across the segments of higher education? In the Fall 1980, the American Council on Education (Andersen and Atelsek, 1982) studied student housing in the nation's 3,037 higher education institutions. More than one-third of all institutions had no student housing, and therefore by previous definitions would be considered 100 percent commuter campuses. An extrapolation from the results of this study shows a distribution of full-time commuter students across different types of institutions as follows: all institutions, 61 percent commuters; public universities, 68 percent; public four-year colleges, 66 percent; public two-year colleges, 76 percent; private universities, 58 percent; private four-year colleges, 41 percent; and private two-year colleges, 50 percent (Andersen and Atelsek, 1982). This is a percentage of *full-time* enrollment. As noted earlier in Figure 1, 41 percent of all undergraduates are part-time students. Thus, if part-time enrollments had been included in the study, the percentages would be even higher. There would be no category of higher education institution that could not be described as having a majority of commuter students as undergraduates.

Unlike describing homogeneous resident student populations, it is not good practice to transfer generalizations about commuter students from one institution to another. Therefore, this complexity makes it essential for institutions to perform their own self-study and research on commuter students and how their needs are served. Then student characteristics can be identified before designing and implementing institutional changes.

References

Andersen, C. J., and Atelsek, F. J. *An Assessment of College Student Housing and Physical Plant.* Higher Education Panel Report, no. 55. Washington, D.C.: American Council on Education, 1982.
Astin, A. W. *Preventing Students from Dropping Out.* San Francisco: Jossey-Bass, 1975.
Astin, A. W. *The American Freshmen: National Norms for 1980.* Washington, D.C.: American Council on Education and University of California at Los Angeles, 1980.
Brodzinski, F. R. "Adult Learners—The New Majority: A Demographic Reality." In A. Shriberg (Ed.), *Providing Student Services for the Adult Learner.* New Directions for Student Services, no. 11. San Francisco: Jossey-Bass, 1980.

Carnegie Council on Policy Studies in Higher Education. Staff consultation report, Washington, D.C., November 1981.

Chickering, A. W. *Commuting Versus Resident Students: Overcoming Educational Inequities of Living Off Campus.* San Francisco: Jossey-Bass, 1974.

National Center for Education Statistics. Staff consultation report, Washington, D.C., November 1981.

Rue, P., and Stewart, S. "Toward a Definition of the Commuter Student Population in Higher Education." *NASPA Forum,* 1982, *2* (6), 8–9.

U.S. Bureau of the Census. *Current Population Reports, "Living Arrangements for College Students: November 1979."* Series P-20, no. 348. Washington, D.C.: U.S. Government Printing Office, 1980.

Sylvia S. Stewart is director of commuter affairs and the National Clearinghouse for Commuter Programs, University of Maryland, College Park.

Penny Rue is assistant director of campus activities, University of Maryland, College Park. A doctoral candidate in College Student Personnel Administration, she is former coordinator of the National Clearinghouse for Commuter Programs.

*A systematic examination of the characteristics of commuter
students and the assessment of an institution's impact on
these students may facilitate needed campus change.*

Institutional Self-Study:
Serving Commuter Students

Rosalind E. Andreas

Cathy the commuter student and Professor Smith have both had long
days. Cathy, frazzled after the dash from work and the fight for a parking space, slips into a dreary classroom trying to quell the inevitable
hunger pangs produced by her lifestyle. Hoping for an early class
break, she recalls that her yogurt is still sitting on her desk at work, the
campus has no evening food service, and no lounge exists in her building. She steels herself for the three-hour lecture and attempts to figure
out how she can get to the library before the next class to rush through
the assigned readings left on reserve. As soon as his class ends Professor
Smith, also tired from a long day of fighting for parking spaces, hunt-
ing for a comfortable corner to enjoy his brown bag with a colleague,
and attending a tedious faculty meeting heads for the babysitter to pick
up his youngest on the way home.

One hopes that the above scenario is not representative of the
collegiate experience for the commuter student or faculty members in
the 1980s. Yet changing national patterns of college attendance over
the past two decades indicate that an overwhelming majority of college
students commute to their classes rather than live on campuses.

S. S. Stewart (Ed.). *Commuter Students: Enhancing Their Educational Experience.* New Directions
for Student Services, no. 24. San Francisco: Jossey-Bass, December 1983.

Depending on which estimate is used, commuter students now out-number their residential counterparts by anywhere from two-, three-, or more-to-one (Trivett, 1974; Educational Facilities Laboratories, 1977; Flanagan, 1976; Rue and Stewart, 1982) and are found in varying numbers at different types of institutions. At the same time, the vast majority of administrators in positions of institutional leadership experienced college as an undergraduate on residential campuses, where they spent most of their time on campus and had abundant opportunities to create a collegiate experience replete with intellectual, social, emotional, cultural, recreational, moral, and educational experiences. The residence halls and student centers provided the comfortable space where people could relax and explore life with peers and faculty. Those same individuals are now administrative leaders at two-year institutions that have 100 percent commuter student populations, urban universities in which the number of residential students tends to be very small, or at major research universities, liberal arts colleges, and state colleges and universities in which the number of commuter students is on the rise.

In contrast, the collegiate experience for many present day commuter students consists primarily of the parking lot, a faculty member in the classroom, a classroom building and its hallways, the registrar's and bursar's offices, and possibly the library and food-service facilities. Many students have been observed studying or eating lunch in their cars, or sitting on the floor in hallways while waiting for a class. As the Educational Facilities Laboratories (1977, p. 6) notes, "Essentially what commuting students lack is a base from which to operate, a place to hang their hats. They need facilities to park their cars and their bicycles, to place their belongings and their children, to study, to grab a quick bite, or take a short nap; they need "hangouts" where they can meet friends or play a casual game of ping pong or pool—in short, places where they feel they belong and can spend time on campus productively." The purpose of this chapter is to investigate the ways institutional leaders can assess the response of their campus to the commuter student. Assumptions about the commuter student are delineated first, followed by a discussion of assessment issues.

Assumptions About the Commuter Student

The National Clearinghouse for Commuter Programs uses the term *commuter student* in reference to any student attending a college or university who does not live in university-owned housing (Jacoby and

Girrell, 1981). That definition encompasses a large group of students, who range in age from the traditional 18-to-23-year-old to the retiree. The student may live at home with parents, in an apartment with a friend, or in a home with a spouse and children. He or she may be fully employed and pursuing career enhancement through additional schooling. Such a definition therefore includes within the commuter student population many subpopulations of students who experience many different lifestages and developmental phases while attending college. Those subpopulations have been characterized as dependent and independent, as well as having part- or full-time status, within the nontraditional age groups (see Chapter One, this volume). In any case, a review of the literature indicates how difficult it is to make generalizations about the commuter student. The time they spend on campus may be brief. Their knowledge of the faculty, university facilities, and even the total campus may be extremely limited. "Rather than envisioning one group, 'the student body,' it is much more nearly accurate to think of commuting students as a very large, independent body of individuals, each one with a set of expectations and needs" (Andreas and Kubik, 1980, p. 3). Nevertheless, there are several generalizations that hold true for most commuter students.

First of all, the commuter student lifestyle can be characterized by a multiplicity of roles. More commuters tend to be employed than resident students (Schuchman, 1974; Harrington, 1972). The age range for commuter students is much broader than that of traditional residential students (Chickering, 1974), and individuals within the commuter population are at many different levels of adolescent and adult development while in school. For these students, higher education competes with work, home, and social interests. Counelis and Dolan (1974) found that family or work environments generally held priority over the educational environment for commuters.

Commuter students also tend to lead a divided life. Much of the literature characterizes their divided lifestyle as due in large part to their multiple roles (Ward and Kurz, 1969; Hardwick and Kazlo, 1973; Chickering, 1974; Schuchman, 1974; Harrington, 1972). Therefore, their social, emotional, and intellectual development occur in different settings than the college or university, with the latter only providing a setting for intellectual development. Commuter students' personal schedules and environmental demands compete with school and prevent them from easily forming friendships with other students, unless there are faculty activities that encourage such interaction (Astin, 1977; Ward and Kurz, 1969; Chickering, 1974). Another generalization that is often true about commuter students is that the time they spend on campus — and therefore the time they commit to higher education in general — is limited. Because work and family commitments tend to be more pressing for commuters than for residential students (Schuchman, 1974; Harrington, 1972; Finkler and Leach, 1978), their time constraints are greater. Such students must allow time for travel to campus (Hardwick and Kazlo, 1973), parenting, and work, and they must plan their schedules around all of the above. Their busy and often inflexible schedules tend to force commuter students to study wherever they can find the time and place (Dressel and Nisula, 1966; Gocek, 1970). In a study of transfer students at an urban university, Scherer (1975) found that many of these students were older, married, and employed, and therefore had developed strategies for allotting time among several competing roles. Many educators view competing priorities on the part of students as a lack of commitment to higher education, but Scherer's findings suggest that such a student in fact may be making a solid, long-term commitment to learning while using strategies to cope with the demands of several different career patterns at the same time.

In general, the commuter-student experience has some common elements, although the group itself is highly heterogeneous. Most commuter students experience the parking facilities, faculty members in their classrooms, the registrar's office, the library, the bookstore, and various food services on campus. Beyond these common areas, the heterogeneity of the commuter population creates a more heterogeneous experience than that of residential students. The returning student may deal with the child care center; the apartment dweller may go to the off-campus housing office; the science major may interact with laboratory assistants; and the musician may confront concert-goers. Commuters' limited and specific experience of the university is probably the main thing these students have in common. But, although commuter students can best be characterized by their heterogeneity, literature on these students prior to the 1960s tended to view this population as generally homogeneous. Then research began to suggest that student affairs personnel were becoming more aware of distinct subgroup differences within the student body (Stodt, 1982; Kuh and Sturgis, 1980; Sedlacek, 1976; Slade and Jarmul, 1975; Astin, 1973; Hountras and Brandt, 1970; Ryan, 1970; Petteway, 1968). In addition, Foster (1978) found that subgroups of commuters differ more from each other than from residential students, concluding that commuters should be considered a heterogeneous group rather than as one similar but amorphous one.

In summary, the commuter student plays many roles in his or her life, leads a divided life, spends a limited amount of time on campus, and has some common experiences with other such students on campus but is often more different from other commuters than residential students. In order for these students to spend quality time on the campus, it is important for them to feel that they belong — even if for only a relatively brief time in their schedules. The commuter student needs to be able to answer questions and solve problems that stem from his or her campus experiences as quickly as possible. Therefore, the accessibility of information, university programs, and personnel are very important to these students.

Assessing the Commuter Student Campus Experience

Recently, I had the opportunity to observe a university senate discussion at an institution that was concluding an academic mission and program review. The participants articulated the institutional intent to strive for academic excellence in a most thoughtful exchange of dialogue. Very conscious of the institution's need for focusing its instructional, research, and public service missions, they spoke of national, state, and regional needs. The institutional intent was to serve the national and international communities through its research, the state through its instruction, and the region through its public service. The governing body debated the merits of sharpening the mission statement to express the institution's intent to be a model university, which served a predominantly commuter student population. A collection of images attached to the terms *commuter campus* and *commuter student* were brought up in the debate. Admissions personnel expressed concern that the "suitcase college" image conflicts with the institution's desired image of excellence. Faculty members voiced the fear that the traditional-age, commuter students were more committed to the latest model automobile than to the goals of academic excellence. Business office and student affairs staff members pointed out that if the image of the commuter campus was highlighted, students might be less likely to choose the residential option because on-campus living might appear less attractive. Other participants expressed a fear that commuter students do not positively identify themselves with the institution but view it as an educational supermarket instead, devoting little time there and providing less institutional support after they graduate. Finally, faculty and student affairs staff alike were concerned that the traditional-age student who lives at home with parents will fail to have the developmental experiences that lead to autonomy expected of a "real" college

14

student. In sum, the discussion implied that the presence of a large commuter student population on campus would ultimately result in an erosion of educational quality.

A study conducted in the mid 1970s at the University of Maryland (Foster and others, 1977) confirms that university personnel hold negative impressions such as those cited above. The researchers studied the question, "Do prejudicial attitudes exist toward students living off campus?" and concluded that place of residence was a significant variable in accounting for differences in attitude toward residential and commuter students. Stamatakos (1980) asserts that this perception is reinforced by the fact that most theories about college student development have been tested on residential populations and that most preparation and training has been focused on residential students almost exclusively (Packwood, 1977; Williamson and Biggs, 1975; Eddy, 1977; Miller and Prince, 1976). Institutions therefore need to analyze the degree to which negative perceptions about the commuter student exist and confront them prior to determining the student development mission for the institution.

With more and more students commuting to campuses, it is important that all individuals who work at a college or university value commuters as well as residential students. Institutional data on the academic performance of commuter students, such as that collected by Hardwick and Foster (1975), can assist in confronting negative attitudes. In addition, the study of student-involvement patterns, on-campus and off-campus employment information, student research-assistant and publication patterns, job placement, and alumni information can do much to dispel misperceptions of commuters. An institutional focus on the diversity of the commuter-student body can set the stage for assessing how well the educational goal of developing better-informed, self-directed, and educated citizens—who contribute to society—is met within the diverse subgroups of that student body. Knowledge of commuter student diversity, success, and achievement can assist administrators specifying the student development mission of their college or university.

Many faculty and staff members have noted that it is always easier to communicate with and learn about the residential than the commuter student. As a result, much remains to be done with commuter students in order to enhance their development. Miller and others (1983, pp. 23–24) assert that "The more student affairs administrators can make available opportunities for commuters to establish campus related reference groups, the more commuters will tend to identify with the campus on a personal and individual basis. The key issue is that all students have developmental lifecycle needs, and the educational enterprise is more than an intellectual supermarket. Personal development is equally important, and higher education will do both students and society a disservice if it does not seek diligently to make experiences of quality equally available to all." Assessing the impact — or lack thereof — of present student services on commuters can identify areas in which these services should change.

The Systems Approach to Institutional Assessment. Once the level of institutional commitment to attracting and retaining commuter students has been decided at a college or university, and misperceptions about the commuter student have been confronted, an examination of how well students, faculty, administrators, alumni, and the community understand the nature of that student can begin. One way to study the accomplishment of institutional mission is to examine the existing academic programs, academic support services, physical plant and facilities, student-development opportunities, and student-service support, to ascertain how well all of these areas create the desired experiences for the commuter student. Because colleges and universities are complex organizations, in which various systems interact to permit the organization to carry out its work, they are best analyzed by using the principles of systems theory (Katz and Kahn, 1978; Lawrence and Lorsch, 1967; Borland, 1983). By dividing a complex system into a hierarchy of subsystems and selecting what needs to be known about a particular subsystem, one can analyze a system without being overcome by its complexity (Seiler, 1967). The analysis can then examine the interaction between the various subsystems.

Student affairs personnel often limit their concern about the commuter student's experience by focusing on support services and programs that complement the academic experience because of the staff's limited area of influence. The same criticism can be levied against any other subsystem perspective or sphere of influence found on a college or university campus. Because higher education places high value on intellectual specialization, its perspective tends to be fragmented into narrow, parochial interpretations that seek to maintain precise definitions. And because of this value, personnel within organizational subsystems tend to hold an isolated, as opposed to an institutional, view of their impact. But a complex organizational analysis, which includes the subsystem views in an integrated rather than an isolated manner, can enhance understanding of the institutional experience. Assessment that accommodates the interaction of the various subsystems within the organization can put the puzzle pieces together into a coherent view of the institution's ability to accomplish its student development mission. As Borland (1983) notes, the complex organizational perspective requires communication networks across subsystems, so that the difference between organizational mission and actual behavior is minimized. Therefore, such a multiple subsystem view can help control for individual subsystem distortions. Communication networks, both formal and informal, are required in order to design the appropriate questions for an institutional assessment.

The Institutional Research Contribution to Analysis. Institutional data, derived from research within institutional subsystems, are required to describe the nature of the student bodies found at the college or university. Answers to such questions as "How many of the students are attending part-time and full time?" and "At what time of day and week are they on or off campus?" are important to an analysis. Campus use will vary of course, depending on the pattern of attendance coupled with other demographic variables such as age, marital status, work pattern, and location. For example, a recent study of graduate students at an urban university found that part-time evening, working, single, or divorced students expressed a strong desire to meet new people (Reisman and others, 1983). Related questions are "From where do the students commute?" "How long is the commute?" (McCully, 1980). The answers could be used in developing off-campus extension sites, public relations and marketing strategies, and public transportation development.

An institutional research study might include queries about which subgroups of students are found in which curricula. One predominantly commuter institution noted that many returning women students were checking "undecided" curriculum codes more frequently than expected. The finding led to an intervention in which women faculty members met with the students to help clarify curricular options (Beardslee, 1976). Another question for an analysis might be "What are the retention and attrition rates of different subgroups of the population?" Information from such a study could highlight groups for which special assistance may be useful (Noel, 1976, 1978; Astin, 1977). That data also could assist admissions personnel in shaping the future student body to meet institutional goals and regional, state, and national needs.

Student Opinions. Use of and satisfaction with campus facilities, programs, and services can be determined from studying the student subsystem. Institutions too often make judgments without asking students and alumni how various aspects of the collegiate experience have affected them. But many campuses have attempted to analyze commuter student satisfaction with the institution's programs. The National Clearinghouse for Commuter Programs attempted to catalogue need-analysis instruments in use at different types of institutions and has listed references annually for those instruments since 1978 (National Clearinghouse for Commuter Programs, 1978). In general, the instruments focus on student perceptions of needed services and satisfaction with existing services. (The design of need-analysis instruments has been addressed for student affairs [Lenning and McAleenan, 1979; Kuh, 1982]; for student program planning [Lenning, 1980]; and for institutional use in general [Scriven and Roth, 1978].) Satisfaction instruments, which allow for specific institutional questions, are available through the American College Testing Program (1970). As an additional service, these satisfaction instruments are normed by institutional type to assist in identifying how an institution's student use and satisfaction with various aspects of the college or university program compare to similar institutions.

Student behavior can also be observed and some assessment experimentation has occurred that uses videotape and photography. Videotaping has been done to determine where students actually study—cars, hallways, empty classrooms, and the library (Burdick and DiFelice, 1980). Photographic evaluation has been discussed as a potential tool for analysis (Collier, 1967; Brown and others, 1980). (For a description of other methods for collecting student-satisfaction data, see Kuh, 1979; Kuh and Sturgis, 1980; Pace, 1969; Pace and Stern, 1958; Webb and Bloom, 1981.)

Faculty and Departmental Administrative Views. Faculty need to determine how well the academic program meets the needs and abilities of the students the institution intends to serve. Academic program reviews of recent years have sought to determine how central each is to the academic mission of the institution, quality of the program, student demand for the program, and institutional costs (Dougherty, 1981; Feeman, 1982; Mingle and Norris, 1981). Faculty involved in such an analysis might ask, "For which commuter students does a given program or academic support system provide a quality experience?"

Similarly, each administrative unit in the college or university should study how well it provides for the students it is intended to serve. Questions for a departmental review of services include: Which students regularly use the programs and services of the unit? Are the policies formulated so that they benefit the student? Do procedures impede or enhance access to the services or programs of the department for these students? Are the resources of the office adequate to meet the needs of the student clientele that the unit is designed to serve? How aware are the staff in the unit under review of the various developmental issues for the subgroups of students served? Is the service or program as designed benefitting the students or is utilization so low that redesign or reallocation of resources ought to be considered?

Institutional Self-Assessment Based on Assumptions About the Commuter Student: An Example

Analysis across the college or university, which considers the many facets of the college experience, can also be conducted by testing how well the university programs reflect the assumptions about the commuter student outlined at the beginning of this chapter. The following chart maps a possible assessment across three subsystems — academic affairs, student services, and administrative affairs. First, an assumption about the nature of the commuter student population is selected. Then an implication of that assumption is identified. Questions are posed for each of the subsystem areas to evaluate their ability to respond to the implication suggested by the assumption. The chart is not intended to be inclusive of all functional areas that might be found in a given division or subsystem unit, but rather serves as a foundation for the development of more complete analysis.

Assessment of the Degree to Which Institution Meets Student Development Needs

Assumption: Time on campus for the commuter student is limited.

Implication: Information about university policies, procedures, programs, and services needs to be accessible and reliable.

Academic Affairs:	Is it possible for students to easily discover when exam periods, graduations, breaks, and early registration periods are held? How is that information disseminated?
	Can students obtain information in advance about course offerings for future semesters?
	Are faculty hours posted in accessible places?
Student Services:	Can students register by phone?
	Are orientations scheduled at several times — day, evening, and weekend? Is it possible to arrive on campus and receive an individualized orientation?

Have parking regulations and services been made explicit and available to each student at the beginning of each semester?

Does the campus provide lockers, rooms, and shower facilities to accommodate the student who must stay overnight occasionally?

How is information about campus activities collected and disseminated? Is it possible for students to plan attendance in advance?

Does the division provide a central information office that one can call to check on events, laboratory and library hours, tutoring assistance, referral sources for problems, and so on?

Is important university information available in the computer system so that when students sign on they will find it there?

Administrative Affairs	Does the personnel unit provide staff training in referral skills?
	Can people easily find campus buildings when they enter the campus, or offices when they enter a building?
	Does the college or university provide payment plan options for students?
	Are campus newspaper stands and racks for other regular publications readily available in high traffic areas and in classroom buildings?

A second implication of the assumption that commuter students have limited time on campus has been identified below and questions are raised for the three subsystems.

Assumption: Time on campus for commuter students is limited.

Implication: Efforts must be made to ensure that the commuter student feels welcome and that he or she belongs on campus.

Academic Affairs:	Does the division provide faculty development sessions that explore ways to involve the learner?
	Have the academic departments created drop-in areas for majors and faculty to talk, relax, and exchange information and ideas?
	Are strong faculty advisers awarded for their efforts in the promotion and review system?
	Are students sought to serve on departmental and college, school, and university governance committees?
	Does the university regularly provide information to faculty about the nature of the student body in a manner that is useful to the faculty?
	Are faculty encouraged to advise student organizations?

Assessment of the Degree to Which Institution
Meets Student Development Needs *(continued)*

Student Services:	Does the orientation program focus assist students in identifying the wealth of college and university resources and also how to connect with the people who help that student to meet his or her goals?
	How easy is it to sign up for racquetball courts and other recreational facilities?
	Are campus activities programmed for particular subgroups of the population and offered at times those students are on campus? Do academic departments cosponsor programs on a regular basis?
	Does the career advising center offer information, counseling, and group seminars to meet differing subgroups' needs for career entry, reentry, retraining, and advancement?
	Does the campus newspaper cover a broad spectrum of issues and their impact on different types of students, or is the media image that of an institution that exists mainly to benefit the traditional-age student living on campus?
	Does the college or university employ a well-trained student advocate, who is well-informed about the diversity of the student body and the developmental issues for the various subgroups of the student body?
	Does the college or university have clearly developed organizational mechanisms for addressing the problems identified by the student advocate?
	How is student leadership training offered? Through weekend retreats, weekly seminars, individualized modules, computerized learning modules available on the mainframe computer, or student development transcript consultation? All of the above?
Administrative Affairs:	Is food service available on evenings? Weekends? In classroom buildings?
	Are classrooms attractive, well-maintained, and inviting?
	Can a student find an attractive, comfortable lounge area in classroom buildings? Are there benches on the campus grounds?
	Is the campus well-lighted at night?
	Does the campus security provide assistance to motorists having difficulty on campus?
	Has the staff development program for employees emphasized concepts and stages in human development, so that employees are attuned to the students, their diversity, and the various developmental tasks that students may experience?
	Do university publications and press releases reflect the diversity of the student body and of campus life?

The approach demonstrated in the above charts can be applied in some detail to functional areas within each of the university subsystems to ascertain how well the college or university is achieving its student development mission. Currently, accreditation for functional areas within student affairs is being addressed by the Council for the Advancement of Standards of Student Services/Student Development Programs (Mable and Miller, 1983). Perhaps that effort and others will make formats for institutional self-studies and assessments more uniform. However, it is important that those efforts use the institution-wide systems approach to assessment — to both increase an institution's understanding of its impact on students and to provide a university-wide base from which to plan program change and resource allocation.

Summary

This chapter has identified means by which institutions can conduct self-studies of their responses to the commuter student. Institutions are encouraged to examine their mission from the perspective of which students they intend to attract, retain, and serve. Given that a college or university has determined to attract commuter students, negative perceptions of such students should be confronted first; then a focus on examples of successful commuters should be emphasized. In addition, a complex organizational perspective for institutional self-study is advocated, as demonstrated by sample institutional-analysis charts based on assumptions about the commuter student outlined in the chapter.

References

American College Testing Program. *The Institutional Self-Study Manual. Part I: Using the Research Results.* Iowa City, Iowa: American College Testing Program, 1970.

Andreas, R., and Kubik, J. "Redesigning Our Campuses to Meet the Needs of Our Commuting Students: Study Lounges." Paper presented at the annual meeting of the American College Personnel Association, Cincinnati, Ohio, April 1981. 25 pp.

Astin, A. W. "The Impact of Dormitory Living on Students." *Educational Record,* 1973, *54* (3), 204.

Astin, A. W. *Four Critical Years: Effects of College on Beliefs, Attitudes, and Knowledge.* San Francisco: Jossey-Bass, 1977.

Beardslee, D. "Majors of Men and Women, 1969 and 1976." Oakland Internal Report Memo, no. 10. Rochester, Mich.: Oakland University Internal Report, 1976.

Borland, D. T. "Organizational Foundations of Administration." In T. H. Miller, R. B. Winston, Jr., and W. R. Mendenhall (Eds.), *Administration and Leadership in Student Affairs: Actualizing Student Development.* Muncie, Ind.: Accelerated Development, 1983.

Brown, R. D., Petersen, C. H., and Sanstead, M. "Photographic Evaluation: The Use of the Camera as an Evaluation Tool for Student Affairs." *Journal of College Student Personnel*, 1980, *21* (6), 588–590.

Burdick, H., and DiFelice, C. Untitled, unpublished videotape of students. Rochester, Mich.: Oakland University, 1980.

Chickering, A. W. *Commuting Versus Resident Students: Overcoming Educational Inequities of Living Off Campus.* San Francisco: Jossey-Bass, 1974.

Collier, J., Jr. *Visual Anthropology: Photography as a Research Method.* New York: Holt, Rinehart and Winston, 1967.

Counelis, J. S., and Dolan, F. A. "Perceptions and Needs: The Full-Time Undergraduate Commuter Student and the University of San Francisco." San Francisco University, Office of Institutional Studies, 1974. 27 pp. (ED 094 611)

Dougherty, E. A. "Evaluating and Discontinuing Programs." In J. R. Mingle and Associates (Eds.), *Challenges of Retrenchment.* San Francisco: Jossey-Bass, 1981.

Dressel, P. L., and Nisula, E. S. "A Comparison of the Commuting and Non-Commuting Student." East Lansing: Michigan State University, 1966. 80 pp. (ED 011 967)

Eddy, J. *College Student Personnel Development, Administration, and Counseling.* Washington, D.C.: University Press of America, 1977.

Educational Facilities Laboratories. *The Neglected Majority: Facilities for Commuting Students.* New York: Educational Facilities Laboratories, 1977.

Feeman, G. F. *Report of the Committee on Academic Mission and Priorities of Oakland University.* Rochester, Mich.: Oakland University, 1982.

Finkler, D., and Leach, M. "Assessment of a University Instructional Evaluation System by Student Consumers." Paper presented at the 62nd meeting of the American Educational Research Association, Toronto, Canada, March 1978, 33 pp.

Flanagan, D. "The Commuter Student in Higher Education: A Synthesis of the Literature." *NASPA Journal*, 1976, *13* (3), 35–41.

Foster, M. E. "A Comparison of Potential Dependent Commuters, Independent Commuters, and Resident Students." *Journal of the National Association of Women Deans, Administrators, and Counselors*, 1978, *42* (1), 40–42.

Foster, M. E., Sedlacek, W. E., and Hardwick, M. W. "The Student Affairs Staff Attitudes Toward Students Living Off Campus." *Journal of College Student Personnel*, 1977, *18* (4), 291–296.

Gocek, M. A. "Library Service for Commuting Students: A Preliminary Study of Problems in Four Southeastern New York Counties." Poughkeepsie: Southeastern New York Library Resources Council, 1970, 28 pp. (ED 037 228)

Hardwick, M., and Foster, M. "Refuting a Myth." *The Commuter*, 1975, *2* (2), 1, 7.

Hardwick, M. W., and Kazlo, M. P. *Designing and Implementing a Commuter Services Program: A Model for Change.* College Park: University of Maryland, 1973. 18 pp. (ED 087 368)

Harrington, T. F. "The Literature on the Commuter Student." *Journal of College Student Personnel*, 1972, *13*, 546–550.

Hountras, P. J., and Brandt, K. R. "Relation of Student Residence to Academic Performance in College." *Journal of Educational Research*, 1970, *63* (8), 351–354.

Jacoby, B., and Girrell, K. W. "A Model for Improving Services and Programs for Commuter Students." *NASPA Journal*, 1981, *18* (3), 36–41.

Katz, D., and Kahn, R. L. *The Social Psychology of Organizations.* 2nd ed. New York: Wiley, 1978.

Kuh, G. D. "Evaluation: The State of the Art in Student Affairs." In G. D. Kuh (Ed.), *Evaluation in Student Affairs.* Cincinnati: American College Personnel Association Media, 1979.

Kuh, G. D. "Purposes and Principles for Need Assessment in Student Affairs." *Journal of College Student Personnel*, 1982, *23* (3), 202–209.

23

Kuh, G. D., and Sturgis, J. T. "Looking at the University Through Different Sets of Lenses: Adult Learners and Traditional Age Students' Perceptions of the University Environments." *Journal of College Student Personnel,* 1980, *21* (6), 483–490.

Lawrence, P. R., and Lorsch, J. W. *Organization and Environment: Managing Differentiation and Integration.* Boston: Harvard University Press, 1967.

Lenning, D. T. "Assessing Student Program Needs." In P. J. Jedamus and M. W. Peterson (Eds.), *Improving Academic Management: A Handbook of Planning and Institutional Research.* San Francisco: Jossey-Bass, 1980.

Lenning, D. T., and McAleenan, A. "Needs Assessment in Student Affairs." In G. D. Kuh (Ed.), *Evaluation in Student Affairs.* Cincinnati: American College Personnel Assocation Media, 1979.

Mable, P., and Miller, T. K. "Standards for Professional Practice." In T. K. Miller, R. B. Winston, Jr., and W. R. Mendenhall (Eds.), *Administration and Leadership in Student Affairs.* Muncie, Ind.: Accelerated Development, 1983.

McCully, B. "On the Need for Separate Commuter Programs: San Diego State Looks at Its Students." *The Commuter,* 1980, *6* (3), 5–7.

Miller, T. K., and Prince, J. *The Future of Student Affairs: A Guide to Student Development for Tomorrow's Higher Education.* San Francisco: Jossey-Bass, 1976.

Miller, T. K., Winston, R. B., Jr., and Mendenhall, W. R. "Human Development and Higher Education." In *Administration and Leadership in Student Affairs.* Muncie, Ind.: Accelerated Development, 1983.

Mingle, J. R., and Norris, D. M. "Institutional Strategies for Responding to Decline." In J. R. Mingle and Associates (Eds.), *Challenges of Retrenchment: Strategies for Consolidating Programs, Cutting Costs, and Reallocating Resources.* San Francisco: Jossey-Bass, 1981.

National Clearinghouse for Commuter Programs. *Index of Commuter Programs.* College Park: University of Maryland, 1978.

Noel, L. "College Student Retention—A Campus-Wide Responsibility." *National ACAC Journal,* 1976, *21,* 33–36.

Noel, L. (Ed.) *Reducing the Dropout Rate.* New Directions for Student Services, no. 3. San Francisco: Jossey-Bass, 1978.

Pace, C. R. *College and University Environment Scales: Technical Manual.* 2nd ed. Princeton, N.J.: Educational Testing Service, 1969.

Pace, C. R., and Stern, G. G. "An Approach to the Measurement of Psychological Characteristics of College Environments." *Journal of Educational Psychology,* 1958, *49,* 269–277.

Packwood, W. T. *College Student Personnel Services.* Springfield, Ill.: Thomas, 1977.

Petteway, S. B. "A Comparison of College Resident and Commuter Students on Selected Psychosocial Characteristics." *Dissertation Abstracts,* 1968, *29* (5A), 1413.

Reisman, B., Lawless, M., Robinson, R., and Beckett, J. "Urban Graduate Students: A Need for Community." *College Student Journal,* 1983, *17* (1), 48–50.

Rue, P., and Stewart, S. "Toward a Definition of the Commuter Student Population in Higher Education." *NASPA Forum,* 1982, *2* (6), 8–9.

Ryan, J. T. "College Freshman and Living Arrangements." *NASPA Journal,* 1970, *8,* 127–130.

Scherer, J. "The Process of Transfer at an Urban University." Unpublished manuscript, Oakland University, Rochester, Michigan, 1975.

Schuchman, H. "Special Tasks of Commuter Students." *Personnel and Guidance Journal,* 1974, *52,* 465–470.

Scriven, M., and Roth, J. "Needs Assessment: Concept and Practice." In S. Anderson and C. Coles (Eds.), *Exploring Purposes and Dimensions.* New Directions for Program Evaluation, no. 1. San Francisco: Jossey-Bass, 1978.

Sedlacek, W. E. "A Comparison of Black and White University Student Commuters." *Journal of College Student Personnel,* 1976, *17,* 134–136.

24

Seiler, J. *Systems Analysis in Organizational Behavior.* Homewood, Ill.: Dorsey Press, 1967.

Slade, T. L., and Jarmul, L. "Commuting College Students: The Neglected Majority." *The College Board Review,* 1975, *95,* 16.

Stamatakos, L. C. "Commuting Students: Theory and Reality from the Professional and Practitioner Perspective." Paper presented at the American College Personnel Association National Conference, Boston, April 28, 1980.

Stodt, M. M. "Psychological Characteristics of 1980s College Students: Continuity, Changes, and Challenges." *NASPA Journal,* 1982, *19* (4), 3–8.

Trivett, D. "The Commuting Student." AAHE-ERIC Higher Education *Research Currents.* Washington, D.C.: American Association for Higher Education, 1974. (ED 090 887)

Ward, R. R., and Kurz, T. E. "The Commuting Student: A Study of Facilities at Wayne State University." Final report of the Commuter Center Project. New York: Educational Facilities Laboratories, 1969.

Webb, E. M., and Bloom, A. "Taking the Student Pulse." *NASPA Journal,* 1981, *18* (3), 25–30.

Williamson, E. G., and Biggs, D. A. *Student Personnel Work: A Program of Developmental Relationships.* New York: Wiley, 1975.

Rosalind E. Andreas is dean of students at Oakland University, Rochester, Michigan. She was the founding chairperson of the American College Personnel Association Commission XVII for Commuter Programs.

An analysis of current practices yields pragmatic advice and working wisdom for those who wish to develop or expand commuter student services.

Organizing for Commuter Student Services

Penny Rue
Jeanne Ludt

The role of student affairs agencies in the enhancement of the educational experience of commuter students takes many forms, depending upon the nature of the student populations served and the educational institutions that commuters attend. Since 1974, the National Clearinghouse for Commuter Programs (NCCP) at the University of Maryland, College Park, has collected various types of information on programs for commuter students and has responded to inquiries from numerous institutions interested in developing commuter student services and programs. In light of these experiences, the NCCP decided to conduct a survey of different types of commuter-oriented student services offices. The results of the survey yield information that can aid institutions interested in developing or expanding programs and services for commuter students.

The decision to establish or reorganize student services with a commuter focus should be based upon careful consideration of institutional mission and goals and a concomitant analysis of student characteristics and needs. The institutional self-study model outlined by

S. S. Stewart (Ed.). *Commuter Students: Enhancing Their Educational Experience.* New Directions for Student Services, no. 24. San Francisco: Jossey-Bass, December 1983.

Andreas in Chapter Two of this volume is recommended as a proce-
dure for arriving at the decision to develop commuter student services.
The focus of the study to be presented here is on the response of student
affairs divisions to commuter student needs. Although valuable services
have been developed by a lone housing or programming staff member,
this study shows that such an approach does not address all of the ways
in which the commuter student's educational experience differs from
that of the traditional resident student. It also fails to respond to the
ways in which the very nature of colleges and universities change as
student populations change. We recommend that commuter student
issues be considered at the very highest policy-making levels of the university, regardless of where those issues are initially raised or ultimately
addressed.

This chapter begins with a look at the origins and development
of commuter student services at twenty institutions. Staff and funding
are analyzed, as well as services and programs. Survey participants
then speak candidly about the progress they have made, the challenges
they face, and the advice they would offer to those developing or expanding commuter student services. The second part of this chapter
highlights some of the creative and cost-effective efforts found at the
surveyed institutions in the various areas of commuter student services.

Methodology

Twenty institutions were selected for participation in this office
models study, based on a National Clearinghouse for Commuter Programs listing of colleges and universities that are known to provide services and programs for the commuter student. A sample of institutions
was developed that represented a cross-section of size, type, commuter
student enrollment, and geographical location. Table 1 lists the institutions and relevant enrollment data. Once selection was made, the
appropriate administrator at each of the institutions was identified, and
a structured telephone interview with him or her was arranged.

Participants were given sufficient time to review the questions
and gather pertinent data prior to their interview. On the average, the
interviews took one hour.

The form and content of the questionnaire were derived from a
review of the general literature on commuter students and descriptive
studies of various programs and offices around the country. The questionnaire was designed to gather information in the following areas:
institutional demographics, title and professional background of inter-

Table 1. Participant Institutions by Enrollment and Proportion of Commuter Students

Institution	Percentage of Commuter Students	Undergraduate Enrollment
Low percentage of commuters	(50 percent or less)	
Boston College	23.5	14,000
State University of New York, Oswego	37.0	7,541
Elon College	38.0	2,480
Hood College	49.0	1,823
Medium percentage of commuters	(50 percent to 75 percent)	
Cornell University	64.0	17,000
University of North Carolina, Charlotte	69.0	9,572
Colorado State University	70.6	19,188
Texas A & M University	71.0	35,000
High percentage of commuters	(75 percent or more)	
Ohio State University	77.0	52,700
University of Maryland, College Park	78.0	29,600
American University	80.0	12,000
University of California, Irvine	80.0	12,000
Oakland University	87.0	11,000
University of Utah	89.3	23,373
Alverno College	92.0	1,334
Wayne State University	95.0	31,241
California State University, Dominguez Hills	96.0	8,279
Cleveland State University	98.0	19,149
Indiana University–Purdue University, Indianapolis	99.5	23,382
Florida International University	100.0	11,885

viewee, origin and history of the office, administrative reporting line, office name and location, office functions, staffing, commuter student role, office funding, methods of communicating with students, and a subjective evaluation of past, present, and future student services efforts. Each question was related to the central purpose of the study: the exploration of the different ways in which people, resources, and environments interact to address the unique student services needs of commuter students. The questionnaire was intended to be broad enough in scope to include colleges that have 25 to 100 percent commuter student populations, especially institutions with a high percentage of commuters. However, we found during the interview process that all questions were not applicable to all institutions. This was particularly true of those campuses with extremely high percentages of commuter students. In those cases, it was difficult to distinguish between commuter services and student services in general.

Origins of Services for Commuter Students

Services and programs for commuter students originated in different ways on the campuses surveyed, based on the historical growth and development of the commuter population itself. Many of the institutions with high percentages of commuter students almost always have been commuter-oriented, and hence have developed a typical spectrum of student services. Examples of such institutions are California State University, Dominguez Hills; Cleveland State University; Indiana University–Purdue University, Indianapolis; and Wayne State University. However, other institutions with high percentages of commuters have not always had commuter majorities and therefore the awareness of the need for services for such students had to be stimulated as the population grew. All of the commuter-oriented offices at such institutions began by focusing on housing, transportation, and other consumer issues. Ohio State University, University of Utah, and Florida International University, all have commuter services that are oriented primarily toward housing and consumer issues. Other institutions, such as Oakland University, have responded to a changing population by reorganizing and developing a comprehensive commuter focus throughout student affairs.

The majority of institutions surveyed began serving commuter students with off-campus housing assistance and are still essentially housing-oriented. Several of these have added a strong programming emphasis, which attempts to educate students about legal issues related to renting property in order to prevent typical problems. Some of the institutions also have become concerned with activities and campus involvement of commuter students. Several of these offices opened in the early 1970s, when students began to move off campus in significant numbers. However, one office cited a starting date as recent as 1980. At two schools, State University of New York, Oswego, and Colorado State University, the students themselves not only originally lobbied for an awareness of commuter students but also continue to fund significant proportions of existing services through student government allocations. At Boston College and the University of Utah commuters are still served under the aupices of the on-campus housing department.

A significantly different approach to beginning programs and services for commuters was cited by some campuses that found themselves educating a changing student population. Hood College, Elon College, The American University, Alverno College, and University of North Carolina, Charlotte, and all schools in which the percentages of commuter students increased rapidly over a short period of time. Administrative initiatives, such as a commuter task force or a student needs assessment, were developed to frame an appropriate response to the new types of students. These institutions began their efforts toward commuter student services with a desire to understand commuters and integrate them more fully into campus life.

Stimulating Institutional Commitment to Commuter Services

Even on campuses that serve commuters almost exclusively it has been necessary to stimulate awareness of the student-as-commuter, because the majority of faculty and staff are themselves products of residential educational experiences. Advocacy of services for commuters is even more critical on campuses where the majority of students were once or are still residents. Staff members surveyed cited a number of strategies that they have employed to raise awareness of these students' needs.

The most popular method for raising awareness is to perform ongoing demographic and needs assessments to determine the numbers and characteristics of commuters and to disseminate this information in a variety of forms to key decision makers and the general campus population. A strong public relations effort—which may include serving on committees, presenting programs, and using the campus media— is the next most frequently employed method. Another popular strategy is to form a staff and student task force or a visible and vocal commuter student association to investigate subtle and not-so-subtle ways that commuters are penalized or ignored and to recommend changes in present programs. Several campuses employ peer counselors and advisers to perform similar functions. Other ways of developing commitment to commuter needs include involving landlords and the general community, lobbying individually with fellow staff members, and producing a variety of information publications.

Philosophy

Participants in the survey were asked to identify their philosophy in working with and for commuter students, and, while these responses varied widely in the way they were articulated, some commonalities exist. The most frequent response was an educational, consumer-oriented focus, that was aimed at empowering students and preventing problems. The next most frequent response was a developmental one that was aimed at determining students' current functioning by assessing their needs and stimulating their growth along developmental models (see Knefelkamp and Stewart, this volume). A strictly service orientation aimed at meeting basic needs was cited by some, and two staff members professed a community development philosophy that was aimed at increasing the involvement of commuters and stimulating cocurricular learning and growth.

Staffing

The number and type of staff varies with the size of the commuter population at the different campuses. All of the institutions surveyed had at least a percentage of a professional staff member's time devoted to commuter issues, all but one funded some clerical assistance, and all but two employed student workers.

Two of the small colleges with relatively low percentages of commuter students, Elon College and Hood College, have a professional staff member who devotes a specified portion of time to commuters. Two institutions with fairly large commuter populations, American University and the University of Utah, also commit part of a professional staff member's time to the needs of these students. Seven of the institutions surveyed have one full-time professional staff member for commuters. In all of these cases, student assistance was available, ranging from one to fifteen students. At three of these, Colorado State, Florida International, and Ohio State universities, the professional staff member is also assisted by two half-time graduate students. All of the institutions with one staff member are oriented primarily toward housing and consumer issues, except for the University of North Carolina, Charlotte, which focuses on social and educational programs to help develop a sense of community among the commuter student population.

Six of the universities in the study have three or more professional staff devoted to commuters and correspondingly have large numbers of commuter students and offer a broad range of services and programs for them. Indiana University–Purdue University, Indianapolis (IUPUI) reported twenty-six professional staff, the highest number of the institutions surveyed; of course since IUPUI is a 100 percent commuter institution, its entire professional student affairs staff was included in that number. The rest of these commuter-oriented schools also depend on large numbers (from ten to eighteen) of student employees, who function as peer counselors, program advisers, office assistants, and even bus drivers. However, as Andreas (1977) notes, some institutions prefer not to designate a particular unit of the college or university to deal with all commuter-related issues but ensure that the various services provided by student affairs staff members — counseling, health care activities, and advising — are accessible to the entire student population.

Administrative Reporting Line

Another approach to the analysis of the staffing of the various student services offices is to examine the level of the staff members within the context of the overall institutional organization. To what department do commuter-oriented staff belong? To whom do they report? Who are their peers? Answers to these questions can illuminate the overall importance of commuter issues on a given campus. As previously mentioned, two of the staff surveyed were members of on-campus housing departments, one an assistant director who reported to an associate director and the other a director who reported to the chief student personnel officer. Three of the respondents were from student activities and student union offices; two reported to union directors and one to the associate dean of student affairs. Therefore, no generalizations can be made about institutional size or proportion of commuters at the institutions as represented by these staff. But eight of the staff members surveyed had titles that contained the words *commuter* or *off-campus*; five of these were in coordinator positions. Two of the eight reported directly to the chief student personnel officers, while the rest were two, three, or four levels removed. All of these individuals reported to people with generalist titles, such as dean of student affairs or director of student development services.

Six of the respondents themselves had generalist titles: One was director of student services, the ranking student affairs staff member on that campus and the rest were some type of dean. Two of these were assistant deans reporting to a dean of students, and the rest reported directly to the chief student personnel officer. All of these generalists represent institutions with high percentages of commuter students. One institution, Colorado State University, defies categorization along these lines. The person with direct responsibility for commuter services was the coordinator of renter's information and had the unique experience of reporting to both the assistant director of housing for apartment life and the vice-president of the student government association.

Funding for Services

It is extremely difficult to analyze trends or models in the area of funding. Although formula funding has been proposed as a general model for student affairs (Maw and others, 1976), it has been criticized for being mechanistic and unrelated to institutional realities. In completing this study, we found that the participating institutions employ a variety of fiscal accounting methods, and that there is little or no consistency in allocations per student or the items included in budget categories. No distinction was made in the survey between total budget and operating budget, and it is difficult to determine whether salaries were included in the figure given. Several of the participants in the study were unaware of their campuses' budgetary procedures. However, staff who operated at the higher levels saw participation in the budget process as a critical vehicle for advocacy and a prime means of garnering additional resources. Commuter-related budgets for the institutions in this survey varied from a low of no operating budget at all and "borrowed" staff time at Elon, to a high at IUPUI of $960,000 a year — the entire student services budget. Most of the other institutions had an operating budget of approximately $20,000, but four of them offered creative programs and services for under $7,000 annually, which did not include professional staff salaries.

Sources of funds were equally varied at the institutions. Most of the offices surveyed received a large portion of their budget from general institutional revenues. However, additional sources of funds had been developed in some cases: (1) across-the-board student shuttle bus fee; (2) user fees, such as for the IUPUI daycare operation; (3) student government association allocations, such as that of the Colorado State Renter's Information Office; and (4) grant funding, such as for the State University of New York (SUNY), Oswego, publications project. Several offices benefitted from the use of student staff who were funded by the college work study program or were able to complete special projects by serving as practicum placements for graduate students.

Collaboration with other offices resulted in the funding of some commuter services projects. "We'll do the work if you'll provide the money" is a strategy that many entrepreneurial commuter services staff have employed. This is a particularly successful approach when producing brochures, handbooks, and other publications; individual departments across campus may not have the time or staff to publicize themselves, or they may be legitimately concerned that their brochure or flyer is often lost amidst the deluge of paper that confronts the student. Departments are often willing to fund a portion of a comprehensive handbook or series of brochures, particularly when distribution to hard-to-reach commuter students is assured. The commuter transportation area is another in which the entrepreneurial approach has paid off, since many campuses are eligible for federal or state funds to promote ridesharing. The personnel and parking management departments have been more than willing to turn funds over to commuter affairs operations, in exchange for publicizing and administering ridesharing programs.

Seeking external funding was an approach employed successfully by several of the offices surveyed, but they described it as being an often frustrating experience. Writing proposals involves a great deal of work initially, with little assurance of success, and many staff are reluctant to risk the time. Most campuses have an office that compiles grant information, and private foundations have also funded student-services projects. The foundations associated with the petroleum industry in particular have been willing to support commuter-oriented proposals. Of course, one of the problems associated with external funding was experienced by several study participants: Their grant funding inevitably expired. Unless there is a reasonable chance that an institution will continue to fund programs when a grant has expired (and this seems increasingly unlikely), it is wise to confine grant-oriented work to specific short-term projects.

Catalogue of Program Functions
Using the SPAR Model

The study participants were asked to chart their activities in services, programs, advocacy, and research (SPAR) using a tally sheet developed by the National Clearinghouse for Commuter Programs and utilized in the Commuter Institution Index (Moore, 1981). SPAR is a comprehensive model for conceptualizing a full range of administrative initiatives on the behalf of commuter students developed by Jacoby and Girrell (1981, p. 37): "In this model one or more units may provide direct *services* to commuter students. Others may concern themselves with *programs* both developmental and recreational in nature, some of which may be designed specifically with the commuter in mind and others of which may be integrative. *Advocacy* functions ensure that the commuter perspective is represented, recognized, and integrated in university-wide planning. All of these should be backed up by *research* on the needs of commuter students, as well as on the outcomes of the various services and programs. Ideally, any or all of the existing elements of a college campus could be involved with one or more of the four SPAR functions." Table 2 indicates the number of institutions offering or participating in the SPAR categories. Items within each category are ranked in order — from most to least number of schools responding to that option.

Services. The three most frequently provided services for commuters are: information center, off-campus housing referral, and carpooling services. These three relate directly to the commuter student's most basic needs for information, housing, and transportation. Most schools also provide lounges and showers and have access to public transportation. Somewhat fewer provide the more complex services of

Table 2. Functions Provided by
Participant Institutions

	Number of Institutions
Services	
Information center	19
Off-campus housing referral	19
Carpool services	19
Shower facilities	18
Lounges in classroom buildings	17
Off-campus bus service	16
Lockers for commuters	15
Child care	13
Special commuter meal plans	12
Preferred parking for carpoolers	7
On-campus overnight facilities for commuters	7
Programs	
Workshops on related topics	19
Programs to promote interaction with faculty and staff	18
Tutorial services for commuters	17
On-campus day social programs for commuters	16
Specialized counseling for commuters	16
Separate commuter orientations	13
Specialized academic advising for commuters	10
Outpost centers in densely populated areas	5
Advocacy	
Part-time employment on-campus for commuters	20
Commuter perspective represented in institutional planning	19
Tenant and landlord legal information	17
Commuter perspective represented in intramural and recreational programming	17
Activities to encourage commuter student participation in:	
Student activities and student government	18
Recreation	15
Traffic policy formulation	14
Health center usage	12
Financial aid policies	10
Research	
Commuter needs assessment	18
Demographic studies of commuters	17
Commuter usage of facilities and services	14
Commuter developmental assessment	10
Longitudinal study	10
Freshman studies only	8
Faculty and staff attitudes toward commuters	3
Commuter and resident student comparisons	3

childcare and specialized meal plans, and less than half offer the more costly preferred parking programs and overnight facilities.

Programs. Programs to meet the diverse educational, cultural, and developmental needs of commuter students are provided at most of the campuses surveyed. Workshops related to the student-as-commuter are offered at all but one institution. Large numbers also provide programs to meet the academic-related needs of students, such as faculty interaction programs or tutoring. Interpersonally oriented social and counseling programs are also offered by the majority of the institutions, but only half offer special academic advising for commuters and only a quarter operate outpost centers.

Advocacy. All of the institutions participating in the study seek to provide on-campus employment for commuters as a method of reducing stress in their lives and providing a vital source of identification with the campus. In addition, almost all of the staff make sure that the commuter perspective is represented in institutional planning and intramural and recreational programming. Tenant and landlord legal information is provided on most campuses as well. Encouraging the participation of commuter students in a variety of aspects of campus life is another advocacy function, which is offered by somewhat fewer institutions. Most schools did advocate for student government and activities participation by commuters. The majority of the institutions encourage participation in recreation, traffic policy formation, and the health center, and half represent the commuter perspective in their formulation of financial aid policies.

Research. Needs assessments are the most routinely performed studies and had been undertaken at all but two of the campuses surveyed, although not necessarily on an annual basis. Most of the institutions also develop demographic profiles of commuter student populations and monitor their use of facilities and services. Half of them have undertaken more complex longitudinal or developmental studies and several perform studies on their freshman class, but only a few of the institutions monitor faculty and staff attitudes toward commuters or perform commuter-resident comparisons.

Communications Services for Commuters

One area of major concern for study participants was how to communicate with commuter students. One of the few generalizations that can be made about commuter students is that they operate outside of the well-developed formal and informal information systems on a campus. Some of the primarily commuter institutions recognize the centrality of this fact and have organized their student services around an information center. But on mixed commuter and resident campuses the information gaps for commuter students are much more noticeable. Commuter students do not receive the mailings sent postage-free to residence hall boxes; they may not see many of the posters and flyers posted around in the most heavily trafficked areas; their radios might not pick up campus stations; and they often arrive at campus too late to get a student newspaper.

Communicating with commuter students usually involves some combination of using existing on- and off-campus media to publicize events and publishing special materials geared toward providing information to commuters. All of the institutions surveyed print posters to inform commuters of events, and all but one publish informative brochures and utilize the on-campus newspaper. A large number publish some kind of handbook, and several assume the cost of mailing information to the commuter's home. A little over half utilize off-campus newspapers and on- and off-campus radio stations. Only a few of the institutions publish a commuter newsletter and take advantage of on- and off-campus television stations.

The Commuter Student Role

Many of the efforts chronicled by this study are directed toward getting commuter students involved in campus life. When the commuter students themselves are involved in lobbying and advocacy, then staff work is augmented substantially. Eighteen of the twenty participating institutions have commuter student representation on key university committees. Twelve have some commuter representation within the student government association, and eleven have a separate commuter student organization. Only seven of the schools have commuter representation at the board-of-trustees level; one has commuter students involved in academic governance. Staff members from eighteen institutions felt that commuter students play a formal role in developing services and programs through lobbying, requests for services, committee work, and assessment processes.

Evaluation of Commuter Services Efforts

Participants were asked several questions that required them to reflect on their commuter student services and programs in a thoughtful and evaluative manner toward the end of the interview. One of the questions concerned the impact their office has had on the campus as a whole, including anything they would like to highlight. The most frequently cited impact was that of increasing awareness within the university community about commuter students and their needs. Not surprisingly, more of the institutions with high percentages of commuters have achieved this objective than those with lower percentages. Roughly half of the institutions in each percentage category mentioned that they have had a positive impact on providing valuable services or programs for their commuter population, particularly in the housing area. Increasing student awareness about the availability of services and programs to help them make the most of their educational experience was cited as an impact by all of the low and medium percentage commuter institutions — but by only one of the high percentage ones. Similarly, almost all of the staff members from institutions with small- and medium-sized commuter populations felt they had developed a sense of community for those students within the larger university context. Of course, most of the institutions with high percentages of commuters have not had to face such problems of attitude and awareness with their populations, since almost all of their students commute.

One area of positive impact that was listed by six of the high-percentage commuter institutions but by only one with a lower percentage is that of increased faculty contact with commuter students. These schools have succeeded in establishing programs in which commuters meet faculty, in sensitizing faculty to commuter student needs, or in improving communication channels among faculty, staff, and students. Staff from several of the institutions that have a consumer-oriented focus report that they are pleased with the impact they have had on landlords in the area, thereby improving the quality of life for their independent commuters. Four staff also mentioned their ability to offer a surprising amount of high quality services with very limited resources.

Accomplishments and Obstacles

Participants in the study were asked to describe particular obstacle that they felt their institutions had overcome — and those that they were still facing — in providing services for commuter students. Those obstacles that participants had surmounted were typical of those achieved in the establishment of any new program: successfully increasing awareness about the service, winning initial budgetary battles such as securing operating funds or new staff members, gaining the respect and cooperation of other campus agencies, and getting the initial critics of a program to change their minds. Other battles that have been won by the institutions surveyed are more specific to commuter services: improving relations with landlords, developing a sense of community among the commuter students, and increasing campus awareness about commuter students.

Many of the obstacles that have yet to be overcome by these

schools will sound familiar to almost anyone working in higher education today: how to increase staff, how to get more funding, how to get more (or better) space, and how to get students to participate. All of these problems were cited by several staff members. Other common hurdles are: recurrent landlord-tenant problems, ineffective communication with commuter students, how to raise awareness about commuter students, and how to develop upper-level administrative support. Less concern was expressed about faculty awareness of commuters, the special problems of dependent commuters, and the public image of the commuter affairs office.

Advice for New Offices

Participants were asked what advice they would give to a colleague who is planning to set up a new office for commuter student services. By far the most popular suggestion was to conduct research, especially needs assessment, in order to create a data base from which programs and services can be planned and for advocacy. The next most frequent suggestion involved using student energy to assist in the development of commuter programs; this response was more frequent among staff from the low- and medium-percentage commuter institutions. Students were found to be helpful in both formal and informal roles, on task forces or as work/study aides, as elected officials, or simply as interested individuals.

Administrative support is deemed equally critical in starting new offices. Experienced commuter services staff members suggest that commuter affairs be placed as high in the organizational hierarchy as possible, to ensure that upper-level administrators become sensitive to the commuter perspective. Without such an awareness, commuter staff members may find themselves and their small budgets bearing the entire burden of meeting the cocurricular needs of commuter students. Also, according to several participants, an initial focus of an office, in addition to advocacy for commuters, ought to be services. Meeting commuter students' basic needs in a timely and reliable fashion can help an office gain tremendous credibility among students, staff, and the community. By adding a problem-prevention focus and by publicizing itself well, a fledgling commuter programs office can develop a solid identity on the campus. Other suggestions from study participants included: developing a broad funding base, beginning with a self-service approach and then employing a developmental approach, and using the resources available through national organizations and professional associations.

Innovative and Successful Examples of Commuter Services

During the course of the study we found that the variety and quantity of functions that can be performed for, with, and on behalf of commuter students is virtually endless. The categories delineated by Jacoby and Girrell (1981) in their SPAR model provide a useful framework for appreciating the types of functions that commuter services staff members perform. However, in reviewing the results of the surveys, two other key factors emerged that seem to have the greatest impact on what actually happens to commuter students on a given campus. Not surprisingly, the first of these factors is level of funding. More services or more complex ones can be offered when more resources, both human and fiscal, are available. But funding is not the sole determinant of what is available on the campuses we studied. Creativity, resourcefulness, initiative, and an entrepreneurial approach on the part of commuter services staff can overcome minimal funds or maximize the use of adequate funds. With these variables in mind, successful, innovative, and unique aspects within the categories of services, programs, advocacy, and research will be highlighted. The following sections provide the reader with examples that illustrate the art of the possible. Although all personnel in higher education are currently frustrated by what cannot be done because funds are limited, it is more productive to focus on what can be done. In fact, given the current emphasis on accountability, a program often must prove its effectiveness before additional funds are granted, regardless of need. As staff members plan for the future, services that appear high in cost should not be discounted, in spite of the present limitations on funding. For example, initially high-cost items such as computers can reduce staff costs overtime. Registration fees, user fees, advertising, and grant funding can all supplement an office's operating budget. By performing a needed function—such as attracting and retaining a new student population—commuter services can justify their growth even when other aspects of the institution are forced to cut back.

Services

There are four principal issues of concern for the commuter student around which services have been developed: (1) housing, (2) transportation to and from campus, (3) consumer services, and (4) access to information. In each of these areas, services can range from the rudimentary and relatively inexpensive to the more complex and costly. In determining which services are most appropriate for a particular institution, Girrell and Jacoby (1981) suggest that two initial questions be considered: (1) What specific services, given institutional limitations and circumstances, can be provided to commuter students? and (2) How can the services already provided be made more accessible to them? In order to help answer these questions, we will present examples of services that can be offered within each of the four areas of commuter student concern.

Housing. Many of the services cited by participants in our study are low in cost, require few staff, and are relatively easy to implement. For example, in the area of off-campus housing referral, many of the institutions surveyed use self-service procedures. In the initial stages of organization, a simple card file is often set up as a source of available housing opportunities. Roommate inquiries can be posted in a similar low-cost fashion by using a centrally located bulletin board. Such a system often is augmented by establishing a communication network with landlords and apartment managers in the community. For many of the offices surveyed it is that liaison with the community that provides an important opportunity to generate off-campus housing listings, as well as to disseminate information regarding tenant and landlord rights or responsibilities. One creative advertising method employed by State University of New York, Oswego, was a "Rent to a Student" poster displayed in stores within the local community.

Many innovative off-campus housing services also exist that require a medium-cost outlay. For instance, housing functions can be expanded to include a rental complaint file and a wall map of the surrounding community. New listings can be cultivated by staff members meeting directly with landlords. In addition, several of the participants gave examples of such supplemental housing services as the availability of pots and pans for loan and a furniture rental package. Commuter student access to these services could be expanded with a minimal increase in funding. For example, at American University as well as several other campuses, the off-campus housing office is kept open during evenings. Commuter student access can also be improved through more and better publicity of the housing services available.

High-cost housing services primarily involve increased complexity of the types of listing described above, professional staff, and/or sophisticated technology. Access to computer technology is the critical factor in increasing the scope of the services that can be offered. This can take the initial form of bound printouts organized, for example, by type of dwelling, geographical location, or cost. Such a system can be upgraded further by using an interactive computer system that provides personalized information for individual specifications. Therefore, a student can type in housing requirements and receive a printout or video display of all available listings that meet those specificiations. Computerizing a roommate locator service in similar fashion is also feasible. Another service that is valuable when a student is searching for a house is a bank of phones in the housing office for use in calling prospective landlords. In addition, an enhancement service offered by some offices in our survey is roommate or tenant and landlord mediation counseling as a means of giving commuter students a formal mechanism for working out problems often encountered in off-campus living. Many of the institutions in the study reported employing peer counselors to minimize the cost of providing counseling services of this sort.

Transportation. Although the issue of locating housing ranks highest on a list of commuter student concerns, meeting transportation needs certainly runs a close second. The lowest cost way of meeting the transportation needs of some students is use of a ride board. In addition, relatively few resources are required to facilitate ridesharing or carpooling efforts. For example, several staff members from the campuses surveyed discussed using a simple grid map or card file for rides on a self-referral basis. In many cases carpooling is made even more attractive by providing preferred parking spaces, which are close to campus buildings, at no extra cost. One valuable transportation service that costs the institution nothing is lobbying public transit agencies for timely and convenient bus and/or train service to and from campus. In addition, commuter students who live close to the campus can be encouraged to use bicycles — if they are provided with secure bike racks near classroom buildings.

Examples of transportation services that are more expensive to implement include a computerized carpool matching system and a campus-based shuttle bus system such as the one developed at the University of Maryland, College Park, which provides both on- and off-campus bus service. However, the cost of providing services such as these does not have to be borne by general revenues but instead can be subsidized by charging user fees, including such a fee as part of the student-fee structure, or receiving government funds for the use of alternative modes of transportation.

Information. Access to accurate information regarding campus life has traditionally been a problem area for commuter students. They are a transient, isolated population by definition, which makes it particularly difficult for the commuter affairs professional to find ways of reaching and involving these students. Nevertheless, those who participated in our survey did not seem to suffer from a lack of creativity or tenacity. Staff from several campuses, including Texas A & M and

University of North Carolina, Charlotte, voiced the importance of developing a regular commuter student column in the campus newspaper. A newspaper column or commuter newsletter can be a powerful instrument for keeping commuters in touch with campus activities and events, as well as providing increased access to information that may have an impact on their daily lives. Although a campus newspaper column may be an excellent low-cost method for disseminating information, it cannot cover as much information as a newsletter. A commuter-oriented newsletter is more costly to produce, but production costs vary depending on whether the newsletter is mimeographed, photocopied, or printed. Advertising can offset the costs as well. Methods of distributing printed information to commuter students include: placing publications in key campus locations, maintaining newspaper boxes in parking lots and at bus stops, using commuter student mailboxes, and mailing directly to the student's residence.

Providing information on campus activities to commuter students can be taken a step further through the use of computer technology. For example, Oakland University has developed a system in which information on campus events is entered into the university's mainframe computer, which provides all students who use the terminals with easy access. Oakland sees word-processing technology as a tool for expanding the number of students reached and the scope of services offered while simultaneously decreasing staff time. Participants from several of the colleges in our survey also mentioned using on- and off-campus radio and television as a means of improving commuter access to information.

In addition to ensuring that the commuter student be provided with up-to-date information on campus activities and events, it is equally critical that standard information be made available to help the student function with greater ease both within and outside the academic community. Standard information is that which varies little in content from year-to-year and is topical in nature. Examples include information on such topics as tenant and landlord rights; rental guides; on-campus eating, sleeping, and study facilities; parking; and transportation. This type of information is most often distributed in the form of handbooks, flyers, brochures, maps, and posters. In each of these cases, the cost is directly related to the production method and the number of copies required. Increased access to standard sources of information can be enhanced through such medium- to high-cost mechanisms as a centrally located campus information center, or a telephone information line such as the one provided by Ohio State University.

Consumer Services. To the commuter student, consumer services play an important role in enriching the quality of campus life, although others on campus might consider such services to be supplemental in nature. Examples of consumer services that are relatively low in cost include access to shower facilities, a commuter student lost-and-found, and an area specifically designated as a commuter student lounge. The majority of institutions surveyed offered at least one or two of these services to their students. American University went one step further and responded to commuter student needs by providing extra study space during exam time. In any case, enhancing the commuter student's educational experience need not be costly or complex. Many of these consumer needs can be met by simply improving access to existing facilities.

Of course, there are more costly forms of consumer services. Commuter student access to lockers is one example of a service that may involve an initially high investment but the cost of which can be offset over time by charging each student a user fee. Another expensive but valuable service is childcare. For commuter students with children, the existence of childcare facilities can be the critical factor in determining whether it is feasible to pursue an education. There are a variety of ways to organize daycare facilities, the least costly of which is a cooperative babysitting service staffed by volunteers. Staff from both Elon College and Cornell University reported having success with this type of childcare facility.

The most elaborate example of a consumer service is the concept of a commuter student center. For example, commuter students at Hood College have their own place to relax, eat, study, and sleep. The existence of a separate facility to meet basic needs of commuter students is extremely helpful and makes a strong statement about the importance of commuter students on the campus.

Programs

Programs, although often supplemental in nature, are office functions that emphasize developmental or recreational enhancement for students. There are essentially three major difficulties encountered in developing programs for commuter students: (1) assessing and meeting the needs of a highly diverse population; (2) finding the most efficient and effective method for publicizing programs; and (3) ensuring adequate commuter student participation. The majority of offices in our study reported having achieved success in overcoming the first two obstacles, but for many the third still remained a problem.

Although commuter students programming is often difficult,

due to the diverse nature of the population, there are numerous reasons for sponsoring such successful programs. A commuter student program has the potential for improving communication both with and among commuter students, as well as providing students with a way to participate in campus life — and usually at low cost. Most programs can be carried out in existing campus facilities with the help of volunteers. Many of the colleges surveyed initiated their commuter programming efforts with an orientation program. Because some of the needs and concerns of commuter students are often very different from those of the residence hall students, there are advantages to scheduling some concurrent orientation sessions. In an effort to be responsive to the whole student population, California State University, Dominguez Hills, has implemented a policy whereby family members also are invited to attend orientation sessions. Topics most often covered during orientation sessions at these institutions include: how to find housing, tenant and landlord information, parking and transportation information, and a description of existing campus facilities and organizations.

The noontime or "brown-bag" concert or lecture series is an additional popular form of commuter student programming. Commuter students are often on campus, available, and looking for a place to go during meal times. Workshops provide another effective forum for increasing commuter student involvement and access to information. Among the campuses surveyed, consumer awareness was cited most often as the focus of commuter student workshops. The following are examples of workshop topics: the housing search, leases, legal rights, energy conservation, transportation, comparative food shopping, roommate selection tips, and security. Other types of innovative programming for commuter students include organized trips to sporting events, off-campus social programs, programs to promote student interaction with faculty and staff, specialized counseling and academic advising available during both regular and evening hours, tutorial services, and commuter student craft and art shows.

Advocacy

Advocacy is one aspect of commuter services that should not be tied to funding. If anything, advocacy efforts on behalf of commuter students are even more necessary at institutions in which funding for commuter student services is low. In any case, advocacy can be as simple as calling the physical plant department when a proposed road closing will block commuter students' access to a parking lot, or as complex as spearheading an effort to change class scheduling procedures and priorities. Advocacy efforts can begin with discussions with all of the student affairs agencies — such as the health center, student union, and the counseling center — to find out what they are doing for commuters at present and to stimulate new ideas.

Several participants stated that advocacy efforts are most successful when grounded in research, so that one has solid data with which to make a case. When a commuter student service office is opened, most of the burden of meeting the needs of commuters may fall to that office, since commuters are often an underserved population. Unless other departments on campus are made aware of their responsibility for serving the needs of commuter students, the efforts of the commuter staff member may not only seem lonely and endless but also may be limited in impact. Shifts in the perspective of the entire campus are needed to provide adequate commuter services and advocacy efforts are often the vehicle for such changes.

One valuable approach to advocacy efforts is linking commuter services with the central mission or goal of the institution (see Chapter Two of this volume), as Hood College has done. Reaching out to new populations for the small liberal arts college often means attracting more commuter students who should be served fully rather than only recruited for their tuition. Public institutions, with a mandate to serve the state's population, seek new learners, many of whom are commuters who deserve a full collegiate experience. Advocacy at the highest levels of university administration may be the most challenging task, particularly for the young professional, but it also has the potential for being the most rewarding.

Ascertaining if all students receive equivalent services and programs in exchange for across-the-board fees has been a powerful lever for making commuter-oriented programming changes at several colleges. Student governments can be strong allies, in fact often leading the charge, in fee-equity issues. And on campuses where student governments provide services themselves, commuter needs have received a great deal of attention. For example, the Student Government Association at University of Maryland, College Park, supports a legal services office with an attorney, paralegal assistant, and student interns. The bulk of their work involves tenant and landlord disputes, and they are active in consumer education and problem prevention. In addition, commuter task forces with representation from all university constituencies, such as the one at University of North Carolina, Charlotte, have made great progress. Task forces not only bring together diverse perspectives in one group, they take this new awareness of different viewpoints back to their peers, therefore acting as advocates in diverse arenas. Also, although faculty are often neglected in student affairs initiatives, linkages with faculty can prove to be among the most valuable in advocating commuter services.

Texas A & M uses a general public relations approach that is helpful to commuter students. High-quality publications, advertising campaigns, and a column in the student newspaper have served to raise the level of the university's awareness of the commuter population. This approach has also given the commuter students a sense of identity and community. Staff at Ohio State University and State University of New York, Oswego, also found that public relations with landlords and transportation providers resulted in improved services to commuters. Often attitudinal barriers or lack of information on the part of critical external agents such as landlords can be overcome with relative ease on the part of staff members.

One simple change advocated by staff on many campuses has had outstanding results: shifting the hours of services and programs to reflect the realities of commuter student lifestyles. Such changes include a noontime music series, evening hours at advising and career planning centers, food service available from early morning to late at night rather than just at traditional meal times, Friday afternoon social mixers, flexible daycare arrangements, and early morning library hours. These changes may require documentation of student needs, desires, or traffic patterns, but have been enacted often on an experimental basis and found to be overwhelmingly successful. Of course, such changes must be publicized to ensure success.

Research

Research should be viewed as the foundation upon which the development of service, program, and advocacy functions rest. As one study participant said, "Don't whine, document." Many student affairs practitioners shy away from research, recalling grueling work done on theses or in research methodology courses. While knowledge of some basic research-design principles is necessary, practitioner research can begin at a very simple level, and a growing body of writing on research addresses this pragmatic need. Once again, funding need not be seen as an insurmountable barrier; some worthwhile information can be gleaned with limited resources.

One assessment method that costs nothing yet is often overlooked is talking with students. Such a method, although informal, can yield a great deal of information and be done in a planful way. Another valuable strategy is using the existing university data bank to obtain information about students, such as place of residence, age, progress toward graduation, and full- or part-time status. The registrar or institutional research office can obtain the data if they are supportive of the way the information is used. Encouraging other offices that routinely administer satisfaction or usage questionnaires to include *place of residence* as a variable and to analyze the results with that as a factor can yield reams of information at no cost to the commuter office. In addition, telephone surveys are inexpensive ways to answer specific questions about students.

Research efforts that require more resources usually involve surveys that need to be printed and mailed, although mailing costs sometimes can be circumvented. Needs assessments, housing surveys, interest surveys, and surveys on the satisfaction and use of a variety of campus services fall into this category. Computer analysis may or may not be needed, but it can often be obtained at minimal cost through the use of students who are looking for experience or class projects. More ambitious studies still can be undertaken at reasonable cost if graduate students carry them out. Graduate students in education, sociology, urban studies, recreation, transportation, and other areas, possibly even from a neighboring institution, are often on the lookout for good research questions. They may be willing to do theses or dissertations on commuter issues, perhaps in exchange for typing, printing, and computer costs.

If resources permit, more ambitious research yields more enlightening data. Studies with large numbers of participants and multiple measures are possible with greater resources. And longitudinal studies that chart some measures over time can be particularly helpful in determining housing trends. Longitudinal and developmental studies chart growth along personal dimensions, and may be interesting in commuter and resident student comparisons. Also, retention studies will increase in importance as traditional student populations diminish, and establishing the links between student services and retention can be powerful in promoting changes in commuter services.

A Developmental Perspective

This study, while offering much pragmatic information about commuter student services, is useful from a different vantage point as well: It illuminates some developmental phases within the growth of the

48

commuter perspective on any campus. When one notes the relative recency of many commuter student service offices, it is heartening to realize that much can be accomplished quite quickly. As the commuter student population grows and diversifies, so do the offices that serve them. Staff, by necessity, become researchers and advocates, developing skills and strategies that have an impact on the entire institution. Additional staff allow a strong programming element to develop, and commuter students themselves may feel a sense of community and identity with the institution. Given current fiscal realities, the pressure to recruit and retain diverse student populations seems likely to increase. In this environment, commuter student services can be a dynamic part of the organizational hierarchy. Therefore, sophisticated commuter student services have developed at many institutions out of necessity — but also because many student affairs practitioners feel that all students deserve the richest educational experience.

References

Andreas, R., and Hillock, B. "Commuter Office Models in Student Affairs." *The Commuter,* 1977, *3* (4), 5–8.

Jacoby, B., and Girrell, K. W. "A Model for Improving Services and Programs for Commuter Students." *NASPA Journal,* 1981, *18* (3), 36–41.

Maw, I. I., Richards, N. A., and Crosby, H. J. *Formula Budgeting: An Application to Student Affairs.* Washington, D.C.: American Personnel and Guidance Association, 1976.

Moore, W. *Commuter Institution Index.* College Park, Md.: National Clearinghouse for Commuter Programs, 1981.

Penny Rue is assistant director of campus activities at the University of Maryland, College Park. A doctoral candidate in College Student Personnel Administration, she is former coordinator of the National Clearinghouse for Commuter Programs.

Jeanne Ludt has a master's degree in College Student Personnel Administration from the University of Maryland, College Park.

The interactions among dependent commuters, their parents,
and their education are extremely important. This chapter
focuses on increasing parental awareness in order to enhance
collegiate experiences.

Parents of Dependent Commuters:
A Neglected Resource

Barbara Jacoby

Commuters have been called the "neglected majority" among undergraduate students on college and university campuses across the nation
(Jacoby and Girrell, 1981, p. 36). Chapter One of this volume breaks
down this highly heterogeneous population by identifying its various
components. Such an identification shows that the groups of students
growing the fastest on campuses — adult, fully employed, part-time,
evening students — are, by definition, commuters. Predictions about
the decline in the numbers of eighteen-year-olds entering college during the next decades and the continued rapid increase in nontradition-
ally aged students abound in recent higher education literature. In
accord with these demographic trends, researchers and educators have
produced a flurry of studies on adult development and services and
programs that address the needs of this emerging population.

Institutions of higher education must respond actively to adult
learners in order to survive the projected decline in the numbers of traditionally aged, full-time students. In addition, it is exciting for student
personnel professionals to plan new services, especially in the context
of new developments in technology that make possible innovations in
communications and service delivery.

S. S. Stewart (Ed.). *Commuter Students: Enhancing Their Educational Experience.* New Directions
for Student Services, no. 24. San Francisco: Jossey-Bass, December 1983.

However, an unfortunate side effect of this growing awareness of older, part-time, and evening students is the assumption that commuters are mainly nontraditional students. Most nontraditional students (those who are over 25 years old) *are* commuters. But the converse — that the majority of commuters on most campuses are nontraditional — is *not* true. In fact, most commuter students are 18-to-22 years old and many live at home with their parents.

Dependent commuters are the silent majority among the overall commuter population. Many of them are present on campus only fifteen-to-twenty hours a week, and they spend almost all of that time in the classroom (Schuchman, 1974). Professionals who work in campus residence halls have long recognized that students spend most of their time out of class in their living situations (Kuh and others, 1983). For dependent commuters, the living situation is generally the parental home.

The Student–Parent Relationship

Researchers who emphasize campus ecology note the importance of the relationship between students and their environment. As Banning (1980, p. 213) states: "The ecological perspective does bring back into focus the concept of campus environments. The concern of student services under the ecological perspective includes the total ecology, the student, the environment, and, most importantly, the transactional relationship between the two." In the case of dependent commuter students, their overall environment extends beyond the campus to include the home. If ecological interactions are defined as those among the various populations in the environment — that is, students with students, students with faculty, and students with staff — the interaction between students and parents also should be added to the list.

With the exception of some private colleges, student affairs professionals traditionally have sought to minimize the role of parents in education and student development. The notion of *in loco parentis*, an early tenet of the profession, seemed appropriate as student personnel staff defined their role as including the responsibility for student shelter, nourishment, health, spirituality, and behavior. This assumption of responsibility coincided with the post-war boom in the building of on-campus residences. However, in the 1960s and early 1970s, the idea of *in loco parentis* faded gradually on some campuses and died suddenly on others (Chait, 1983). As student affairs took on less regulatory, less parental objectives, *individual development* became the key defining term.

But the profession did not return this role to parents. On the contrary, they became further disassociated from their students' education by the implementation of provisions of the Buckley amendment, which restricted parental access to such information as students' class schedules, grades, and health records. However, given the major influence parents have on students — particularly dependent commuters — the student affairs profession probably has done students a disservice by virtually excluding parents' participation in their children's higher education experiences. This chapter focuses on increasing parental association with students' education in order to enhance collegiate experiences.

To begin with, I will describe briefly several typical dependent commuter situations in terms of parental relationships and the reasons these students have for living at home while attending college. These situations are clearly not mutually exclusive, since they are only examples; in fact, it is very possible that several are applicable at the same time to most students.

First of all, economic constraints, coupled with cutbacks in federal student financial aid, require growing numbers of students to live at home even if they would prefer campus residence. In some of these cases, the forced close proximity of students to their parents may breed hostility on one or both sides. Students may feel trapped and that their sense of independence is stifled by living with their parents. They may react by spending inordinate amounts of time outside of the home. Parents, on the other hand, may feel guilty and hold themselves responsible for hampering the student's ability to take full advantage of being in college.

Some students find themselves attending college largely or even primarily as a result of parental pressure. These students often come from families that, as a result of ethnic, racial, and/or economic considerations, have not sent anyone to college in previous generations (Schuchman, 1974). In a 1980 national sample of freshmen, 45 percent of the fathers and 53 percent of the mothers of the students had had no college experience (Astin, 1981). Parents who never went to college may see higher education as a means of improving their child's social or economic status. The pressure to succeed may be greatest in the cases of parents of first-generation college attenders in certain ethnic, class, or religious groups, who may believe in virtually absolute control of parents over children. In contrast, some students from lower socioeconomic backgrounds may go to college against the wishes of their parents, who do not see the value or usefulness of higher education. Such students may see a college degree as their means of gaining a more affluent lifestyle. Therefore, parents may be favorably or unfavorably disposed toward their children's desire for upward mobility.

In another example, family obligations may account for a major portion of the physical and emotional energy of students who live at home. Parents, especially those of first-generation college students, often continue to demand the same responsibilities for household chores and other activities as the student held while in high school. In rural settings this may entail significant amounts of farm labor. Indeed, at peak planting and harvesting periods, students who reside on family farms may be absent regularly from classes. In other cases, students are responsible for the care of an infant, elderly, or disabled family member. In single-parent households, college students may assume additional domestic duties that restrict their ability to participate in campus life.

Another group of dependent commuters is composed of students whose past academic performance forces them to attend open-admission institutions. This situation is often coupled with financial limitations that preclude their living on campus. Related factors such as poor high school grades and aptitude test scores, as well as heavy dependence upon family financial resources and entitlement grants, may result in low self-esteem and low self-confidence on the students' part regarding their ability to succeed in college. These students frequently are in particular need of their parents' encouragement and support.

Less mature individuals may find themselves in the dependent student category because any of a variety of emotional ties keep them at home. These students sometimes describe these ties as financial. However, lack of funds is often not the determining reason for their remaining at home: They may feel that their parents will forget them. Others may fear that their departure will cause discord that could destroy the family structure (Schuchman, 1974). Individuals who have not had the opportunity to venture far from their home environment may find the prospect of leaving it frightening. Thus, they remain where they feel secure with their familial role, neighborhood, and high school friends.

Of course, students may simply choose to live at home because it is the optimal living situation. They are satisfied with feeling comfortable in their home situation and participating in the opportunities available to them at their college or university.

Dependent Commuters Compared to Resident Students

It is not surprising that commuter students living at home are more likely than resident students to experience conflict with their parents

(Burnett, 1982). Studies also reveal that commuters, in comparison with residents, conform more often to parental expectations (Kysar, 1964) and are more emotionally dependent on their parents (Schuchman, 1974). Sullivan and Sullivan (1980) found that dependent commuters exhibited less affection, communication, satisfaction, and independence in their relationships with parents than resident students. Graff and Cooley (1970) also show that commuter students demonstrate poorer mental health, curricular adjustment, and less maturity in defined goals and aspirations than residents. As a result of these factors, commuters in general have been found to have less self-esteem and more psychosomatic symptoms when compared with resident students (Lundgren and Schwab, 1979).

Dependent commuters tend to participate in extracurricular activities at relatively low levels because they remain quite involved in relationships and activities in and around the home (Chickering, 1974). Transportation difficulties and employment are also factors that discourage such participation. Furthermore, Astin (1977) shows that full-time students living with their parents are less likely than residents to complete their degree in four years. Carney (1980) confirms that commuter students have a significantly lower graduation rate compared with all other students. As Chickering concludes (1974, p. 84), "Students who live at home with their parents fall short of the kinds of learning and personal development typically desired by the institutions they attend."

In light of some of the findings cited above, student development specialists such as Chickering have urged that institutions attempt to minimize the disadvantages of commuter students by explicitly building short-term residential experiences into the educational plans of students. While on-campus residence may be desirable, it is unlikely that many institutions will be able to respond in this manner. Therefore, concentrating on the improvement of home and campus environments in order to raise the level of satisfaction with college felt by dependent commuters, and to increase the likelihood of their completing their education, is a more readily achievable goal.

Developing Parental Involvement

The campus-ecology perspective is helpful in emphasizing the importance of the interaction between students and their living environment (Aber, 1983). This approach promotes adjustment in the environment as a legitimate way to respond to student needs (Banning and de Martinez, 1983). The campus ecology perspective assumes the participation of all campus community members, including students, faculty, and administrators (Kaiser, 1975), and calls for a major shift in attitude, skills, and training (Banning, 1980). In applying the ecology concept to dependent commuters, parents must be included in the model. Student services professionals can affect the environment of these students by building parental identification with the student's college or university, by increasing parental understanding of the educational process, and by creating an active role for parents in fostering their children's development. The remainder of this chapter describes ways in which parental involvement may be increased, ranging from strategies that foster passive affiliation to those that require a high level of participation.

Building Parental Identification. With little investment of resources, student affairs staff can do quite a bit to encourage parents to feel more positive about the institutions their children attend, which in turn will give positive reinforcement to the students. Conscious efforts on the part of the institution to build parental identification are especially critical in communities where most parents have not attended college and ties to local high schools may be particularly strong. Parents of first-generation college students, who may question the value of college, can develop resentment against their son's or daughter's new affiliation. However, the proverbial ounce of prevention can go a long way in fending off such feelings of resentment. Admissions staffs should involve parents in recruitment efforts at the high school level, such as by sponsoring "college nights." If the institution offers preadmission campus visits, parents should be encouraged to attend. And, once a student has been admitted, a letter from a highly placed campus official is in order. Such a letter can congratulate parents on the admission of their son or daughter and invite the family to become part of the campus community.

Many colleges and universities hold special functions that may be a part of orientation activities to introduce parents to the campus and key administrators. These functions may range from formal receptions in the president's home to casual outdoor gatherings in which all family members are welcomed. Of course, the nature, time, and location of such events all heavily influence attendance. For example, some rural institutions have found that replacing a late-afternoon tea that includes a receiving line with a pot-luck supper or an outdoor barbecue dramatically increased the number of parents in attendance. Institutions with religious affiliation may find that an activity following a Sunday church service would be well received. In addition to official meet-and-greet functions, campuses often invite parents to get a taste of collegiate life by organizing "parents' days" or "parents' weekends." On these occasions, parents may be asked to attend specific athletic or cultural events, as well as to tour and dine on campus. Student services professionals may do well to consult with the alumni office staff, who generally are quite experienced in organizing this type of activity.

There are many other ways to foster closer ties between parents and the institution. The initial letter to parents upon the student's admission could be accompanied by an invitation to visit the campus and information that renders that invitation less intimidating, such as the location of visitor parking, menus and hours of campus food services, and popular items that are available in the bookstore. Parents could receive regular announcements of campus sports, entertainment, and cultural events by direct mail or through local media. Reduced rates for students' families would be an added inducement for them to attend such events. With a little creative forethought it is possible to take advantage of already scheduled mailings in order to share or avoid postage expenses. For example, 1983 income tax checks from the state of Maryland were accompanied by applications for season tickets to the upcoming University of Maryland football games. Along this line, small businesses generally are willing to sponsor the production and distribution of items that help build identity with local institutions if the items are useful in promoting their own services or products. These may include bumper stickers, tee-shirts, pennants, and even imprinting shopping bags with a university logo and intercollegiate athletic schedules, as done at a food store in Lexington, Kentucky.

Frequently, colleges and universities offer a variety of services to the surrounding community. Informing parents of the availability of such options as noncredit courses, information and research facilities in the agricultural and extension services, health care, legal clinics, counseling and testing, and childcare and preschool opportunities can make them feel that the campus is concerned with their needs as well as those of students. In addition, parents can be made to feel a part of the campus community through the formation of parents' associations. Parents may be invited to dine in the homes of faculty and staff or to attend receptions or banquets at which students are honored for superior academic, leadership, and other achievements. Moreover, parents should be considered as more and more institutions rely on community volunteers to supplement their paid staffs.

Informing Parents About the Institution. In addition to creating a sense of affiliation for parents, it is important to provide them with a broad range of information about the institution. This may be accomplished in several ways. Most colleges and universities offer

56

some sort of orientation program for parents, which may run separately or jointly with the student program. However, according to the National Orientation Directors Association 1982 Data Bank (Bailey and Clement, 1982), no parent orientation is available at 22 percent of all institutions with fewer than 5,000 students, at 17 percent of institutions with between 5,000 and 15,000 students, or at 10 percent of institutions with over 15,000 students. In planning parent orientations, careful thought should be given to scheduling Saturday and evening programs so that working parents may attend. If planners suspect that transportation and parking present impediments to parent participation, it may be worthwhile to provide bus transportation. A less costly alternative would be to assist parents in arranging carpools. At a minimum, these basic topics should be covered in parent orientation: academic information (courses of study, registration, grading, and credits); services and facilities; finances and sources of aid, including employment; transportation; extracurricular offerings (organizations, activities, and honors).

However, even at institutions that have well-developed parent orientation programs, a large number of parents do not attend—by choice or because of unavoidable conflicts. Parents who do not participate are perhaps those who could most benefit from the experience. Thus, outreach efforts should be conducted in conjunction with on-campus programs. These may be in the form of direct-mail information, perhaps supplemented by the provision of one or more taped messages that parents can have access to by dialing special telephone numbers. Also, orientation meetings can be held in off-campus settings such as community centers, high schools, and libraries. And a campus information booth can be set up at community fairs and in shopping centers.

Helping Parents Understand the Stresses of College Life. Getting parents to identify with their child's college or university and providing them with comprehensive information so that they can avoid the frustration of having only fragmented bits of knowledge about the institution can certainly increase the likelihood of favorable parental disposition toward the student's college attendance. Nevertheless, most parents, especially those who have not themselves attended any institutions of higher education, will have little understanding of what college involves today—in terms of social and intellectual challenges, decision making, and study requirements. Therefore, in order to assist parents in becoming a source of support for students, the parent orientation function should be expanded beyond the provision of institutional information to encompass an explanation of the typical stresses of college life. These should be described in a positive light, as resulting from natural student growth patterns or phases, not as crises or problems. Topics that have the effect of creating or deepening parental appreciation of the collegiate experience include: transition to the institution and the many differences between high school and college; role conflicts that may result from the contrast between the institutional and the home environments; need for quiet and privacy in the home; areas of difficulty that are frequently encountered (dealing with the bureaucracy, academic changes, feeling confused by the myriad of options and opportunities available, and feeling overwhelmed by the amount of class preparation required); pressures to make major and career decisions; and the need for emotional support from parents.

As mentioned in the last section, parents who have little understanding of such issues may be the least inclined to attend an orientation program at which these issues are discussed. Parents whose children are the first generation to attend college may feel especially threatened. A newsletter sent to parents at predictable student stress points — for example, prior to the first semester, at midterm time, and before final exams — could help them become aware of the strains the student may be experiencing and of how they can be supportive. If direct mail is too costly, an alternative might be to convince the local newspaper to print a regular or occasional column for parents of college students and, specifically, of dependent commuters.

Smaller or community-based institutions may want to consider organizing neighborhood meetings of parents to discuss their own adjustments to and experiences with children who are college students. Parent support groups may be particularly effective if organized by faculty or staff members who are themselves parents of college students. Along the model of parent-teacher associations, parents may be invited to visit the campus during the semester, to attend one of the student's classes, and to meet an instructor on an informal basis.

Teaching Parents to Be Paraprofessionals. One of the seemingly unbridgeable gaps between the college experience of commuter and resident students has been that residents have the benefit of living in an environment staffed by professionals trained to understand their conflicts, support them in facing challenges, and foster their development. Student services professionals can help dependent commuters gain some of these benefits by actively inviting parents to participate in the development of their son or daughter and by providing them with the skills they need to do so (Bieber and others, 1983). If the profession

58

readily trains students to act as paraprofessionals in the residence halls, why not offer similar training to parents of dependent commuters? Specific areas that could be covered in training programs are: the maturational tasks of college students (such as dealing with authority, developing autonomy, managing emotions, maintaining self-esteem, and establishing identity); stage models of late adolescent and early adult development; predictable crises; risk-taking behavior, such as experimentation with drugs and the use of alcohol; interpersonal relationships and sexuality; career decision making; basic listening and counseling techniques.

Possible formats for paraprofessional training for parents may range from a session that is part of a parent orientation program or a one-day workshop to an on-going seminar or even a credit or noncredit continuing education course. Trainers could be counselors, student affairs staff, faculty, and/or students. Methods could include readings, lectures, videotapes of actual or simulated situations, and role-playing.

Since so many factors in the dependent commuter's situation may seem to pose obstacles to parental involvement in the student's college experience, student services professionals need to take the initiative in establishing and enhancing that involvement. The student's participation in higher education has the potential for creating a bond within the family and being a source of stimulation rather than inducing conflict and resentment. Using parents as a resource also expands the scope of the student services professional's efforts to improve the quality of life for commuters who live at home. Furthermore, institutions that establish strong relationships with students' families may reap the considerable benefits—financial and otherwise—of the good will of their parent constituents.

References

Aber, G. W. "Campus Ecology." *NASPA Forum,* 1983, *3* (7), 9–10.

Astin, A. W. *Four Critical Years: Effects of College on Beliefs, Attitudes, and Knowledge.* San Francisco: Jossey-Bass, 1977.

Astin, A. W. *The American Freshman: National Norms for Fall, 1980.* Washington, D.C. The American Council on Education and the University of California at Los Angeles, 1981.

Bailey, B., and Clement, L. (Eds.). *National Orientation Directors Association Data Bank, 1982.* College Park: National Orientation Directors Association, Orientation Office, University of Maryland, 1982.

Banning, J. H. "The Campus Ecology Manager Role." In U. Delworth, G. R. Hanson, and Associates (Eds.), *Student Services: A Handbook for the Profession.* San Francisco: Jossey-Bass, 1980.

Banning, J. H., and de Martinez, B. M. B. "Diversity: An Ecological Perspective." *The Campus Ecologist,* 1983, *1* (1), 2.

Bieber, J. P., Fullerton, N. J., Pierre, K. M., and Tootle, B. J. "Commuter Student Development: Parents as Paraprofessionals." Paper presented at the American College Personnel Association Convention, Houston, March 1983.

Burnett, D. "Traditional-Aged Commuter Students: A Review of the Literature." *NASPA Forum,* 1982, *2* (7), 6–7.

Carney, M. *Persistence and Graduation Rates of Greek, Independent, Commuter, and Resident Hall Students: A Nine Semester Study.* Norman: Office of Student Affairs Research, University of Oklahoma, 1980.

Chait, R. "Student Affairs Strategies in an Age of Education, Not Regulation." *Chronicle of Higher Education,* 1983, *26,* 88.

Chickering. A. W. *Commuting Versus Resident Students: Overcoming Educational Inequities of Living Off Campus.* San Francisco: Jossey-Bass, 1974.

Graff, R. W., and Cooley, G. R. "Adjustment of Commuter and Resident Students." *Journal of College Student Personnel,* 1970, *11* (1), 54–57.

Jacoby, B., and Girrell, K. W. "A Model for Improving Services and Programs for Commuter Students." *NASPA Journal,* 1981, *18* (3), 36–41.

Kaiser, L. R. "Designing Campus Environments." *NASPA Journal,* 1975, *13* (1), 33–39.

Kuh, G., Hanson, G., and King, P. "Assessing the Quality of Student Life—Commission IX." Paper presented at the American College Personnel Association Convention, Houston, March 1983.

Kysar, J. E. "Mental Health in an Urban Commuter University." *Archives of General Psychiatry,* 1964, *11,* 472–483.

Lundgren, D. C., and Schwab, M. R. "The Impact of College on Students." *Youth and Society,* 1979, *10* (3), 227–235.

Schuchman, H. "Special Tasks of Commuter Students." *Personnel and Guidance Journal,* 1974, *52* (7), 465–470.

Sullivan, K., and Sullivan, A. "Adolescent-Parent Separation." *Developmental Psychology,* 1980, 16 (2), 93–99.

Barbara Jacoby is assistant director of the Office of Commuter Affairs at the University of Maryland, College Park. She is also assistant director of the National Clearinghouse for Commuter Programs and a member of the directorate body of the American College Personnel Association Commission XVII (Commuter Programs).

The successful application of development theory to commuter
students requires challenging some long-held assumptions.

Toward a New Conceptualization
of Commuter Students:
The Developmental Perspective

L. Lee Knefelkamp
Sylvia S. Stewart

The previous chapters in this sourcebook have reviewed successful
research and programming efforts for and about commuter students.
We hope these discussions provide good examples for readers to follow
and encourage a broad-based commitment to an institution's responsibility for educating commuter students. In addition, this chapter calls
for an examination of our assumptions about commuter students and a
reconceptualization of our attitudes toward them.

Commuters as Different, Not Deficit

This chapter is based in part on the work of Carol Gilligan,
which encompasses both a critique and a challenge of traditional
models of human development. Her most recent work, *In a Different
Voice: Psychological Theory and Women's Development* (1982), discusses

S. S. Stewart (Ed.). *Commuter Students: Enhancing Their Educational Experience.* New Directions
for Student Services, no. 24. San Francisco: Jossey-Bass, December 1983.

seven assumptions that have powerful implications for the application of developmental theory to commuter students. The review of data on commuter students contained in the other chapters of this sourcebook indicates that there are marked similarities between the research on and institutional response to commuter students and Gilligan's conceptualization of women and accompanying human development models. For example, commuter students comprise 80 percent of the nation's undergraduate population (Rue and Stewart, 1982), yet they are often referred to only alongside resident students. In addition, the single most salient characteristic of commuter students is their diversity. The commuter population includes traditional- and nontraditional-age students; undergraduate and graduate students; full- and part-time workers; Cross' "new students," first-generation college attenders whose past academic experience has been difficult (Cross, 1976); second-degree students; career changers; and continuing education students. Yet that same diversity often is used as a rationale for excluding commuters from research samples; their very complexity is problematic for most research designs. In any case, this chapter addresses the following assumptions often made about commuter students:

- The definition of being a college student traditionally has been equated with living in residence halls.
- The residence experience is considered the normative experience of college students.
- The characteristics associated with resident students are positive and reflective of all student development. (This assumption may be due to the cumulative effect of three factors: (1) Many early studies of student personality development were based on characteristics of resident students; (2) the undergraduate experience of many college and university faculty and staff was residential; and (3) many graduate programs unwittingly perpetuate the assumption that residence on campus is the norm.)
- The characteristics associated with resident living facilitate development and are attributed exclusively to resident living, as opposed to being attributed to other campus-based activities as well.
- Commuter students are analyzed in terms of their differences from residence students, and as a group, are considered to reflect maturational deficits rather than logical and predictable individual and group differences.

The characteristics of commuter environments have not been

studied as intensively as resident environments, in part because of the assumption that commuter environments do not facilitate development, and also because of the difficulty of studying such complex environments. However, commuter students should be studied in all of their diversity and complexity, because such studies will legitimize their experiences. And the knowledge gained will help correct and expand our notions of college student development. To date, equating residence students with normal development and their environments with optimal developmental settings, while excluding commuters and their situation has resulted in misperceptions about both populations and a lack of well-designed research studies. But studying commuter students and their characteristics as well as other groups usually omitted from analyses, such as graduate and international students, can enhance understanding of the complexities of the college student.

Commuter from Deficit to Assets

A reconceptualization of the commuter student can change what traditionally has been viewed as a problem in research and programming into an array of research and practice possibilities. This new perspective can be an asset in the way we think about our students and our practice in general. Several illustrations of how commuters can be viewed as an asset to institutional research rather than a deficit are listed below.

- As a group, commuter students represent sociological and political issues as well as developmental and maturational ones. These issues should be separated so that commuter students' sociological differences are not confused with their maturational differences. Research on commuters therefore can provide new information in both domains.
- As new research on commuter students is conducted, it will become necessary to include both human development models and local campus-based data in the formulation of research design and interpretation.
- Research models to use with commuter student populations should also include adult transition models, such as those of Schlossberg (1981) and Neugarten (1976), along with the more traditional models of student and personality development.
- Studying the maturation process of commuter students may illuminate qualities of maturity that are not illustrated by the

lives of resident students, such as the ways in which they prioritize values, time, and roles. Commuter students' struggles with autonomy and intimacy certainly should be explored.

• Since the majority of staff, faculty, and students in the higher education community are commuters, we should look to learn from research on such a broad-based population rather than just to study it.

Commuters from Asset to Institutional Change

Viewing commuters, or any students, as assets when they have previously been viewed as deficits allows the practitioner to create possibilities for institutional change. Tables 1 and 2 have been designed as general models, based on some of our observations and understanding of existing data about commuters. They can be used as a guide to assessing environments or populations. In fact, many of the suggested changes could benefit the general population. Such an assessment includes at least five steps from the "Practice-to-Theory-to-Practice" model of assessment and design by Wells and Knefelkamp (1981): (1) Definition of the population and environment; (2) careful observation and listing of the populations' needs and the environmental press, defined as an individual or group interpretation of a situation, stimulus, or event (Walsh, 1973); (3) determination of the existent student characteristics and environmental conditions; (4) evaluation of the interaction between the need and the press to determine if that interaction is facilitating or inhibiting; (5) creation of an action plan for movement from what already exists to a changed environment.

Table 1. Commuter Students in the Higher Education Environment: The Needs-by-Press Interaction

The Traditional-Age Commuter Student (Needs)	The Higher Education Environment (Press)
Commuter students possess characteristics that are both similar and dissimilar to resident students.	Commuter students often are viewed as the same as residents and no program adjustments are made; or they may be seem as so different that many of the qualities they have simply because they have chosen to be students are ignored.
Commuter students need to be recognized, legitimized, understood, and deserve an institutional response.	Commuter students are often neglected; the image of the college student is that of the resident student.

Table 1. *(continued)*

(Needs)	*(Press)*
Commuter students are not a uniform →The campus environment tends to type. They can best be characterized ← treat all commuter students the same by their heterogeneity.	way.
Commuter students have developmental and maturational skill-building needs, as well as service needs.	Programs for commuter students frequently center around services, such as transportation and housing.
Commuter student interests may revolve around multiple roles and are not necessarily centered on the campus.	Competing priorities for a student's time often are seen as a lack of commitment on the student's part to higher education.
With many roles and responsibilities, commuter students are likely to have developed high levels of instrumental autonomy.	Intellectual autonomy is reinforced and recognized more frequently than instrumental autonomy on campus; encouragement for independence in nonintellectual domains is often incidental.
Commuter students expect good teaching and structured identification of tasks and processes.	Faculty care about good teaching, but generally are not trained in teaching skills; class goals and tasks are often not explicitly outlined.
Commuter students expect vocational preparation and skill development that will lead to a good job.	Few attempts are made to relate classroom learning to vocational preparation or potential career applications.
Commuter students may need flexibility in schedules to complete assignments, courses, and degree programs.	Programs and academic calendars are usually inflexible and are built around specific units (semesters, quarters, and so on).
Commuter students live in communities away from the campus.	Programs and outreach are done primarily on-campus. Facilities and services often are not available in the evenings or early AM hours and are not in "satellite" offices in the offered community.
Commuter students have a great need for a clear, precise campus information system, both formal and informal.	The decentralized structure of most campuses means that information dissemination is scattered or frequently by word of mouth.
Commuter students have a great need for meeting places that afford social opportunities, or are quiet settings for studying and relaxing.	If such spaces exist, they often are only in one central place, like a student union.

Table 1. *(continued)*

(Needs)	*(Press)*
Commuter students have a need for → opportunities often associated with ← residence on campus — more time with faculty, more intensive peer interaction time, and a closer integration of their living and learning experience.	Most opportunities to meet interpersonal needs are informal, outside of the classrooms, and require student initiative. In institutions with large commuter populations, opportunities to establish relationships may be more limited or difficult.
Commuter students often remain exclusively embedded within their high school peer culture or previous family patterns.	Most opportunities for campus involvement in cocurricular activities assume a prior affiliation with a structured, formal, campus group.
Commuter students live in communities as citizens. These communities place demands and responsibilities on students and therefore afford them citizenship rights.	Higher education tends not to acknowledge this citizenship as legitimate and does not assist in making linkages between classroom learning and these off-campus opportunities.

Source for table format: Barna and others, 1979.

Table 2. Commuter Students in the Higher Education Environment: Challenges for Student Personnel Administrators

Student affairs staff members face the challenge of designing programs that provide commuter students with more supportive environments. Several ways that professional staff can meet this challenge are identified below. While some functions involve working with specific offices, they also can be seen as challenges to all agencies to share in the creative design of environments and programs that enhance the commuter student's educational experiences.

Function	*Challenge*
Faculty Consultation	• Develop an educational partnership to assist faculty in the design of more effective learning environments that include alternative teaching modes, nontraditional learning options, and deliberate developmental curricula
Research	• Conduct and report research on the characteristics and needs of commuter students • Develop and report interventions and models that address these needs • Expand research on the characteristics of college and university environments

Table 2. *(continued)*

Function	Challenge
Campus Awareness	• Articulate commuter student presence, needs, concerns, characteristics, and expectations throughout the educational community
Program Design	• Design social, cultural, and recreational programs that challenge and support commuter students in the environment and capitalize on their strengths
Advising	• Structure career and academic advising to help with realistic major and career choices and supplement the teaching-learning environment
Orientation	• Design campus environments that are easier for commuter students to negotiate; reach out to high schools and parents to prepare students for maximizing the benefits of university experiences
On-Campus Employment	• Encourage access to and design new campus employment opportunities for commuter students that foster connections with their coursework and facilitate their involvement with the campus community
Facilitate Maturity	• Create opportunities for commuter students to develop skills in leadership, values clarification, and responsible citizenship
Facilities Management	• Design and maintain lounge, study, recreation, and eating spaces that encourage interaction at decentralized locations
Physical and Psychological Services	• Develop health service models that accommodate diverse needs and schedules but also foster health based on medical, health education, and physical development
Scheduling	• Arrange classes, services, and events at times and in locations that assist the student's ability to take advantage of offerings
Information	• Create unbiased and equitable presentations of generic information about academic and service offerings of the campus
Financial Monitoring	• Investigate and produce models of equitable determination of financial need and distribution of financial aid resources

Source for table format: Barna and others, 1979.

Conclusion

We began this chapter with serious questions about the subtle yet powerful assumptions that bias much of the work on commuter and resident students. We suggested that studying commuter students produces a more adequate description of the characteristics associated with college student development in general and with commuters in particular. A large base of knowledge concerning models of personality development and a limited number of research studies on commuters exists. A growing body of literature also addresses the assessment and redesign of campus environments, including Aulepp and Delworth, 1976; Banning and Kaiser, 1974; and Huebner, 1979. These should be studied in order to inform our analyses of students — and the actions that a responsible college or university will take to meet student needs. We believe practitioners should use this knowledge in combination with their own daily observations of students and campus environments.

We also maintain that the attempt to study and respond to the needs of traditional-age commuters can serve as a process model for attempting the same with other diverse groups whose voices have not been heard and who are often considered to be deficits in institutional research — that is, adult learners, new students, minorities, and women. Finally, we need to focus on those environmental conditions that facilitate development and accept the responsibility for changing or designing such supportive environments. Erik Erikson (1959) has suggested five characteristics of a qualitative environment: (1) experimenting with multiple roles; (2) experiencing meaningful achievement and decision making; (3) being free from excessive anxiety (physical and psychological); (4) experiencing choices; and (5) having time for introspection and reflection. Erikson's characteristics are listed here because we think they apply to almost any environment, whether it be a classroom, residence hall, committee meeting, or union program. In addition, the previous charts have attempted to provide concrete illustrations of how these concepts can be applied in the design of programs and environments for commuter students.

In general, beside collecting data about commuter students, we need to change our attitudes toward them. We hope that such an attitude change will help student services staff take responsibility for institutional change, thus enhancing the educational experience for all students.

References

Aulepp, L., and Delworth, U. *Training Manual for an Ecosystem Model: Assessing and Designing Campus Environments.* Boulder, Colo.: Western Interstate Commission for Higher Education, 1976.

Banning, J. H., and Kaiser, L. "An Ecological Perspective and Model for Campus Design." *Personnel and Guidance Journal,* 1974, *52*, 370–375.

Barna, A., Haws, J. R., and Knefelkamp, L. L. "The New Student: Challenge to Student Affairs." Paper presented at the American College Pesonnel Association Convention, Los Angeles, March 1979.

Cross, K. P. *Beyond the Open Door: New Students to Higher Education.* San Francisco: Jossey-Bass, 1976.

Erikson, E. H. "Identity and the Life Cycle." Psychological Issues Monograph, vol. 1. New York: International Universities Press, 1959.

Gilligan, C. *In a Different Voice: Psychological Theory and Women's Development.* Cambridge, Mass.: Harvard University Press, 1982.

Huebner, L. A. (Ed.) *Redesigning Campus Environments.* New Directions for Student Services, no. 8. San Francisco: Jossey-Bass, 1979.

Neugarten, B. "Adaptation and the Life Cycle." *The Counseling Psychologist,* 1976, *6* (7), 16–20.

Rue, P., and Stewart, S. S. "Toward a Definition of the Commuter Student Population in Higher Education." *NASPA Forum,* 1982, *2* (6), 8–9.

Schlossberg, N. "Adult Transitions." *The Counseling Psychologist,* 1981, *9* (2), 2–16.

Walsh, W. B. *Theories of Person-Environment Interaction: Implications for the College Student.* Iowa City: American College Testing Program, 1973.

Wells, E. A., and Knefelkamp, L. "A Process Model of Practice-to-Theory-to-Practice." Staff development presentation, Old Dominion University, February 1981.

L. Lee Knefelkamp is associate professor of counseling and personnel services at the University of Maryland. She is also faculty associate for student development in the Division of Student Affairs. Her work focuses on the use of developmental theory in the design of learning environments and student personnel programs.

Sylvia S. Stewart is director of commuter affairs and the National Clearinghouse for Commuter Programs at the University of Maryland, College Park.

Related organizations, general readings, and examples of practice for those interested in improving services for commuter students are recommended.

Sources of Additional Information

Sharon L. Taylor
Sylvia S. Stewart

Related Organizations

The following organizations can provide additional information and contacts with other professionals who work with commuter student concerns.

American College Personnel Association (ACPA) Commission XVII on Commuter Programs. In 1978 the Commuter Task Force became ACPA's newest commission: Commission XVII (Commuter Programs). Its purpose is to create a network of support for understanding and developing programs and services that enhance the educational environment of the commuter student at institutions of higher education. The commission focuses on four special areas: (1) promoting student development; (2) conducting research regarding commuters; (3) providing professional support to those working with commuters; and (4) developing linkages with other professionals and groups concerned with commuter issues. These goals are achieved through a national newsletter; conference presentations at the local, state, regional, and national levels; periodic publications by commission members; and a network of interested professionals who provide assistance to one

S. S. Stewart (Ed.). *Commuter Students: Enhancing Their Educational Experience.* New Directions for Student Services, no. 24. San Francisco: Jossey-Bass, December 1983.

another. Those interested in joining Commission XVII should send their names, titles, institutions, addresses, telephone numbers, ACPA/APGA membership numbers, and any specific areas of interest to: Jeanne Likins, Commission XVII Chairperson-elect, Assistant Dean of Students, American University, 200 M.G.C., Washington, D.C. 20016.

National Association of Student Personnel Administrators (NASPA) Commuter Institution Network. NASPA members with a special interest in the commuter campus have formed a network with the following stated purposes: encouraging collaborative research among commuter institutions; engaging in cooperative efforts with other professional associations that deal with issues related to the commuter student; providing a mechanism for the exchange of information and ideas among professionals concerned about commuter students; encouraging programs and publications that deal with issues related to commuter students; providing information to student personnel leaders about the impact of commuter students on college and university campuses. NASPA members who have an interest in participating in the activities of the network are encouraged to write: Dana Burnett, Dean of Student Affairs, Old Dominion University, Norfolk, Virginia 23508, or Sylvia S. Stewart, Director of Commuter Affairs, 1195 Adele H. Stamp Union, University of Maryland, College Park, Maryland 20742.

The National Clearinghouse for Commuter Programs (NCCP). The primary focus of the clearinghouse is on students in higher education who do not live in institution-owned housing. NCCP was created to share data concerning characteristics and needs of commuter students and to establish channels of communication among schools interested and involved in services, programs, advocacy, and research for the student living off campus. Some of the resources and services the clearinghouse provides for members are: *The Commuter,* a quarterly newsletter; "References on Commuting Students," a bibliography of relevant literature on commuter students and commuter institutions; "Commuter Institution Index," a compendium of programs and services offered by clearinghouse constituents; a referral service for linking individuals who have specific concerns with others who have established programs in response to similar concerns; liaison with ACPA Commission XVII, Commuter Programs. Those interested in joining should write: National Clearinghouse for Commuter Programs, 1195 Adele H. Stamp Union, University of Maryland, College Park, Maryland 20742.

General Readings

Astin, A. W. *Preventing Students from Dropping Out.* San Francisco: Jossey-Bass, 1975.

Chickering, A. W. *Commuting Versus Resident Students: Overcoming Educational Inequities of Living Off Campus.* San Francisco: Jossey-Bass, 1974.

Chickering, A. W., and Associates. *The Modern American College: Responding to the New Realities of Diverse Students and a Changing Society.* San Francisco: Jossey-Bass, 1981.

Cross, K. P. *The Missing Link Connecting Adult Learners to Learning Resources.* New York: College Entrance Examination Board, 1978.

Cross, K. P. *Adults as Learners: Increasing Participation and Facilitating Learning.* San Francisco: Jossey-Bass, 1981.

Cross, K. P. "Planning for the Future of the Student Personnel Profession." *Journal of College Student Personnel,* 1981, *22* (2), 99–104.

Flanagan, D. "The Commuter Student in Higher Education: A Synthesis of the Literature." *NASPA Journal,* 1976, *13,* 35–41.

Gelwicks, L. E., and Weinstock, R. "Managing the Environment for Older Students." In H. H. Kaiser (Ed.), *Managing Facilities More Effectively.* New Directions for Higher Education, no. 30. San Francisco: Jossey-Bass, 1980.

Harrington, T. F. "Commuter Students in Urban Colleges." In S. E. Goodman (Ed.), *Handbook on Contemporary Education.* New York: Bowker, 1976.

Hodgkinson, H. *Guess Who's Coming to College: Your Student in 1990.* Washington D.C.: National Institute of Independent Colleges and Universities, 1983.

Huebner, L. A. (Ed.). *Redesigning Campus Environments.* New Directions for Student Services, no. 8. San Francisco: Jossey-Bass, 1979.

Lynch, M. L., and others. *Student Affairs in the 1980s: A Decade of Crisis or Opportunity?* Ann Arbor, Mich.: ERIC Clearinghouse on Counseling and Personnel Services, 1981.

Moore, B. *References on Commuting Students.* Third ed. College Park, Md.: National Clearinghouse for Commuter Programs, 1981.

Nuver, M. E. *The Characteristics and Needs of Nontraditional Students: An Annotated Bibliography of Data-Based Literature (1950–1980).* Cleveland, Ohio: Cleveland State University, 1981.

Peterson, D. A. *Facilitating Education for Older Learners.* San Francisco: Jossey-Bass, 1983.

74

Quay, R. H. *On the College Student as an Individual: A Bibliography of Arthur W. Chickering.* Public Administration Series, bibliography P-823. Monticello, Ill.: Vance Bibliographies, 1981.

Rue, P., and Stewart, S. S. "Toward a Definition of the Commuter Student Population in Higher Education." *NASPA Forum,* 1982, *2* (6), 8–9.

Schlossberg, N. K., and Entine, A. *Counseling Adults.* Monterey, Calif.: Brooks/Cole, 1977.

Shriberg, A. (Ed.). *Providing Student Services for the Adult Learner.* New Directions for Student Services, no. 11. San Francisco: Jossey-Bass, 1980.

Trivett, D. A. "The Commuting Student." AAHE-ERIC/Higher Education *Research Currents.* Washington, D.C.: American Association for Higher Education, 1974. (ED 090 887)

Examples of Practice

Aikman, C. C. "Problems Beyond the Golden Door: Refugees and the Commuter Campus." *Lifelong Learning: The Adult Years,* 1982, *5* (8), 11, 27.

American Association of State Colleges and Universities. *Alternatives for Later Life and Learning: Some Programs Designed for Older Persons at State Colleges and Universities.* Washington, D.C.: American Association of State Colleges and Universities, 1974.

Andreas, R., and Hillock, B. "Commuter Office Models in Student Affairs." *The Commuter,* 1977, *3* (4), 5.

Andreas, R., and Kubik, J. "Redesigning Our Campuses to Meet the Needs of Our Commuting Students: Study Lounges." Paper presented at the annual meeting of the American College Personnel Association, Cincinnati, Ohio, April 1981.

Arthur, S. "Designing a Student Government to Suit a Community Institution." *The Commuter,* 1977, *3* (4), 1.

Arthur, S. "Designing Ways to Serve the Commuting Student." *Liberal Education,* 1977, *63* (2), 316–321.

Association of College and University Housing. *Off-Campus Housing — A Survey of ACUHO Member Institutions.* Ithaca, N.Y.: Association of College and University Housing, 1980.

Bauer, W. K. "Strategies for Recruiting and Retaining the Nontraditional Student." *College Student Journal,* 1981, *15* (3), 234–238.

Bishop, J. B., and Snyder, G. S. "Commuters and Residents: Pressures, Helps, and Psychological Services." *Journal of College Student Personnel,* 1976, *17,* 232–235.

Blodgett, J. E., and Lewis, J. M. "The Mentor Advising Program." *The Commuter,* 1982, *7* (2), 1.

Braun, R., and Lease, T. "The Relevancy of the ACU-I Role Statement to Commuter/Two-Year Colleges." *Conference Proceedings, Association of College Unions-International,* April 1975, 12–15.

Bridwell, M. "An Opinion on Today's College Health Centers." *The Commuter,* 1983, *8* (2), 1.

Bryant, P. S. "I Am Curious (Adult): Building Programs to Attract Adult Students." *CASE Currents,* 1980, *6* (11), 26–28.

Burton, B. H. "Preadmission Day for Older, Nontraditional Students." Paper presented at the annual convention of the American Personnel and Guidance Association, Detroit, Michigan, March 1982.

Carlson, J. "Programming for the Off-Campus Student." *The Bulletin, Association of College Unions-International,* 1981, *49* (5), 4.

Christensen, V. *Organization and Operation of a Child Care Center at the University of West Florida.* Pensacola, Fl.: University of West Florida, 1977.

Conyne, R. K. "The Campus Change Advocate." *Journal of College Student Personnel,* 1977, *18* (4), 312–316.

Danglade, J. K. "Support Services for Off-Campus Part-Time Students: The Total University Approach." *Adult Leadership,* 1977, *25* (6), 169–177, 188.

Desiderio, J. "Promotional Programming for Evening Students." *The Commuter,* 1977, *4* (1), 6.

Educational Facilities Laboratories. *Housing for New Types of Students.* New York: Academy for Educational Development, 1973.

Educational Facilities Laboratories. *The Neglected Majority: Facilities for Commuting Students.* New York: Educational Facilities Laboratories, 1977.

Euculano, J. M., and Andreas, R. "Adapting Technology for Management in Commuter Affairs." *The Commuter,* 1982, *8* (1), 3–4.

Felton, H. F. "Sports Clubs at Commuter Colleges." *Journal of Physical Education and Recreation,* 1978, *49* (2), 48–49.

Florio, C. *Collegiate Programs for Older Adults: A Summary Report on a 1976 Survey.* New York: Academy for Educational Development, 1978.

Foster, M. E., Sedlacek, W. E., and Hardwick, M. W. "Student Recreation: A Comparison of Commuter and Resident Students." Research Report 4-77. College Park: Counseling Center, University of Maryland, 1977.

Frisz, R. H., and Aylman, C. E. "Publicity and Promotion of Student Activities Programs at an Urban Commuter Campus." *Journal of College Student Personnel,* 1980, *21* (5), 460.

Future Directions for a Learning Society. *350 Ways Colleges Are Serving Adult Learners.* Princeton, N.J.: College Board Publications, 1979.

Garni, K. F. "Urban Commuter Students: Counseling for Survival." *Journal of College Student Personnel,* 1974, *15,* 465–469.

Gentry, R. "Commuter Advisor Program." *The Commuter,* 1974, *1* (3), 2.

Gertz, F. "Opportunities Available to Lessen Cost of Ridesharing Programs." *The Commuter,* 1979, *5* (1), 5.

Girrell, K. W. "Off-Campus Housing: The State of the Art." *The Commuter,* 1980, *5* (3), 3.

Glass, J. C., Jr., and Hodgin, H. H. "Commuting Students and Cocurricular Activities." *Personnel and Guidance Journal,* 1977, *55* (5), 253–256.

Gribbon, R. *Commuter Students: A Challenge for Ministry.* Washington, D.C.: The Alban Institute, 1978.

Grimmett, R. "Programs That Work for Commuter Students." Paper presented at National Association of Women Deans, Administrators, and Counselors Conference, April 1975.

Hardwick, M. "Priority Program Game: Identifying Commuter Counseling Needs." College Park: National Clearinghouse for Commuter Programs, University of Maryland, 1974.

Hardwick, M., and Kazlo, M. "Designing and Implementing a Commuter Services Program: A Model for Change." Commuter Research Report, no. 3-73. College Park: Office of Commuter Services, University of Maryland, 1973.

Hardwick, M., and Kazlo, M. "Services and Facilities Available to Commuter Students." *Journal of College Student Personnel,* 1974, *15,* 225.

Hardwick, M., and Knefelkamp, L. L. "Innovations in Commuter Orientation: A Simulation Experience Based on Student Development Theory." Paper presented at National Association of Women Deans, Administrators, and Counselors Convention, March 1976.

Harrison, L., and Entine, A. "Existing Programs and Emerging Strategies." *The Counseling Psychologist,* 1976, *6* (1), 45–59.

Hatala, R. J. "Some Thoughts on Reaching the Commuting Student." *Liberal Education,* 1977, *63,* 309–315.

Heffernan, J. M. *Educational and Career Services for Adults.* Lexington, Mass.: Heath, 1981.

Hyde, W. "Commuting Costs for Community College Students." *Journal of Student Financial Aid,* 1980, *10* (3), 11–18.

Jacoby, B. "Housing Hunters: An Orientation Session for Housing Seekers Off Campus." *The Commuter,* 1980, *5* (2), 3.

Jacoby, B., and Girrell, K. W. "A Model for Improving Services and Programs for Commuter Students." *NASPA Journal,* 1981, *18* (3), 36–41.

Jacoby, B., and Likins, J. M. "Reaching Out to Commuter Students." *The Orientation Review,* National Orientation Directors Association, 1980, *10* (3), 4.

Kaplan, D., Barr, V., and Galassi, J. "An Outreach Program with Students Older than Average." *Journal of College Student Personnel,* 1981, *22* (4), 375–376.

Lenz, E. *Creating and Marketing Programs in Continuing Education.* New York: McGraw-Hill, 1980.

Levy, L. C. "Adelphi on Wheels." *Change,* 1976, *8,* 25–28.

Lienemann, W. H., and Smith, A. E. "College in the City: Commuters and Community Houses." *Improving College and University Teaching,* 1974, *22,* 55–56, 58.

Magoon, T. M. "Student Life and the Task of Counseling in Colleges and Universities in the 1980s." Research Report, no. 17–80. Paper presented at the Counseling Seminar, Japan Association of Student Counseling, Tokyo, November 1980.

McCoy, R. D. "Commuter College Orientation: The Walkthrough." *Journal of College Student Personnel,* 1973, *14* (6), 551.

McGraw, L. W. "A Selective Review of Programs and Counseling Interventions for the Reentry Woman." *Personnel and Guidance Journal,* 1982, *60* (8), 469–472.

Makler, R. H. "Identity Confusion, Satisfaction with Campus Environment, and Related Variables as Factors in Participation in Student Activities at an Urban Community College." *Dissertation Abstracts International,* 1977, *37* (12-A, Pt. 1), 7544–7545.

National Clearinghouse for Commuter Programs. "How to Travel to Campus? Transportation Information: A Resource Listing from the Clearinghouse." *The Commuter,* 1977, *3* (2), 1.

National Clearinghouse for Commuter Programs. *Commuter Institution Index.* College Park: University of Maryland, 1981.

National Clearinghouse for Commuter Programs. "Peddling Programs: Getting the Message Across." *The Commuter,* 1981, *7* (1), 6.

Nichols, D. D. "Community College Health Service Programs: A Progress Report." *Journal of American College Health Association,* 1979, *27,* 184–187.

Nordberg, J. "Commuter Center Operates Daycare Facilities." *The Bulletin,* Association of College Unions-International, 1977, *45* (3), 7.

Okun, M. (Ed.). *Programs for Older Adults.* New Directions for Continuing Education, no. 14. San Francisco: Jossey-Bass, 1982.

Pappos, A. V. "Traveling Road Shows: An Outreach Strategy in Counseling." *Journal of College Student Personnel,* 1978, *19* (1), 74–75.

Pennington, W. D., and Keller, M. H. "Program Primer for 'Road Scholars'." *Student Activities Programming,* 1982, *15* (4), 28–32.

Perkins, L. "Project Tel-A-Friend (Orientation at Purdue-Calument)." *The Commuter,* 1977, *3* (2), 6.

Pitman, R. "Evening Commuters: Priorities for Student Services." *The Commuter,* 1979, *4* (4), 1–3.

Rich, H. E., and Jolicoeur, P. M. *Student Attitudes and Academic Environments: A Study of California Higher Education.* New York: Praeger, 1978.

Rue, P. "How to Give 'Em What They Want: Assessment Basics for Commuters." *The Commuter,* 1981, *7* (1), 1.

Rue, P. "Program Development: A Model That Works." *The Commuter,* 1981, *7* (1), 2.

Rue, P. "Communicating with Commuters." *The Commuter,* 1982, *8* (1), 1.

Shotzinger, K. A., Buchanan, J., and Fahrenback, W. F. "Nonresidential Advisors: A Peer Counseling Program for Commuter Students." *NASPA Journal,* 1976, *13,* 42–46.

Streeter, R. B. "Alternative Financial Resources for the Nontraditional Student." *Journal of Student Financial Aid,* 1980, *10* (2), 71–22.

Suddick, D. E., and Owens, L. "The Adult College Student: What Development Educational Services Do They Desire?" *College Student Journal,* 1982, *16* (1), 89–91.

Tristan, M. P., Cheney, C. C., and Novelli, W. J., Jr. "A Descriptive and Analytic Study of the Student Health Services of an Urban University." *Journal of the American College Health Association,* 1978, *26* (5), 268–271.

U.S. Department of Transportation. *Ridesharing Programs of Educational Facilities.* Washington, D.C.: Federal Highway Administration, 1982.

Vaughan, G. B. "Learning in Transit at Mountain Empire Community College." *Community and Junior College Journal,* 1974, *44,* 54–55.

Voit, S. "Providing Legal Services to Students Living Off-Campus." *The Commuter,* 1980, *5* (2), 1.

Waterhouse, P. G. "Commuter Orientation: Is It 'Is' or Is It 'Isn't'?" Special Report no. 1-75. College Park: National Clearinghouse for Commuter Programs, University of Maryland, 1975.

West, J. H., and Ray, P. B. "The Helper Therapy Principle in Relationship to Self-Concept Change in Commuter Peer Counselors." *Journal of College Student Personnel,* 1977, *18,* 301–305.

Wills, B. S., and Ross, J. "Food Service and Residence Hall Facilities Being Offered to Commuters by Member Institutions of ACUHO." *Journal of College and University Student Housing,* 1976, *6,* 13–16.

Sharon L. Taylor is coordinator of the National Clearinghouse for Commuter Programs, University of Maryland, College Park.

Sylvia S. Stewart is director of commuter affairs and the National Clearinghouse for Commuter Programs, University of Maryland, College Park.

Index

A

Aber, G. W., 53, 58
Advocacy, function of, 33, 34, 35, 44–46
Aikman, C. C., 74
Alverno College, and student services, 27, 28–29
American Association of State Colleges and Universities, 74
American College Personnel Association (ACPA), 71–72
American College Testing Program, 17, 21
American Council on Education, 7
American University, and student services, 27, 28, 29, 40, 43
Andersen, C. J., 7
Andreas, R. E., 2, 9–24, 26, 30, 48, 74, 75
Arthur, S., 74
Association of College and University Housing, 74
Astin, A. W., 3, 6n, 7, 11, 12, 16, 21, 51, 53, 58, 73
Atelsek, F. J., 7
Aulepp, L., 68, 69
Aylman, C. E., 75

B

Bailey, B., 56, 58
Banning, J. H., 50, 53, 54, 58, 68, 69
Barna, A., 66n, 67n, 69
Barr, V., 77
Bauer, W. K., 74
Beardslee, D., 16, 21
Beckett, J., 23
Bieber, J. P., 57, 59
Biggs, D. A., 14, 24
Bishop, J. B., 74
Blodgett, J. E., 74
Bloom, A., 17, 24
Borland, D. T., 15, 16, 21
Boston College, and student services, 27, 28
Brandt, K. R., 12, 22
Braun, R., 75

Bridwell, M., 75
Brodzinski, F. R., 3, 7
Brown, R. D., 17, 22
Bryant, P. S., 75
Buchanan, J., 78
Buckley amendment, 51
Burdick, H., 17, 22
Burnett, D., 53, 59, 72
Burton, B. H., 75

C

California, Irvine, University of, student services at, 27
California State University, Dominguez Hills, and student services, 27, 28, 44
Carlson, J., 75
Carnegie Council on Policy Studies in Higher Education, 6n, 8
Carney, M., 53, 59
Chait, R., 50, 59
Cheney, C. C., 78
Chickering, A. W., 3, 8, 11, 22, 53, 59, 73
Christensen, V., 75
Clement, L., 56, 58
Cleveland State University, and student services, 27, 28
Collier, J., Jr., 17, 22
Colorado State University, and student services, 27, 28, 30, 31, 32
Commuter Institution Index, 33
Commuter students: assessing campus experience of, 13–18; assumptions about, 10–13, 62; campus time limited for, 12, 18–20; challenges of, 66–67; definition and distribution of, 3–8, 10–11; dependent, 5–6, 49–59; developmental view of, 61–69; as different, 61–63; divided life of, 11; environments for, 68; examples of practice for, 74–78; as heterogeneous group, 12; and institutional change, 64–67; as institutional research assets, 63–64; institutional self-study for, 9–24; by institutional type, 7; multiple roles of, 11; myths about, 4–5, 13–14;

Statement of Ownership , Management, and Circulation
(Required by 39 U.S.C. 3685)

1. Title of Publication: New Directions for Student Services. A. Publication number: USPS 449-070. 2. Date of filing: September 30, 1983. 3. Frequency of issue: quarterly. A. Number of issues published annually: four. B. Annual subscription price: $35 institutions; $21 individuals. 4. Location of known office of publication: 433 California Street, San Francisco (San Francisco County), California 94104. 5. Location of the headquarters or general business offices of the publishers: 433 California Street, San Francisco (San Francisco County), California 94104. 6. Names and addresses of publisher, editor, and managing editor: publisher — Jossey-Bass Inc., Publishers, 433 California Street, San Francisco, California 94104; editor — Ursula Delworth, Gary R. Hanson, University of Iowa, Counseling Center, Iowa City, Iowa 52242; managing editor — Allen Jossey-Bass, 433 California Street, San Francisco, California 94104. 7. Owner: Jossey-Bass Inc., Publishers, 433 California Street, San Francisco, California 94104. 8. Known bondholders, mortgages, and other security holders owning or holding 1 percent or more of total amount of bonds, mortgages, or other securities: same as No. 7. 10. Extent and nature of circulation: (Note: first number indicates average number of copies of each issue during the preceding 12 months; the second number indicates the actual number of copies published nearest to filing date.) A. Total number of copies printed (net press run): 2658, 2670. B. Paid circulation, 1) Sales through dealers and carriers, street vendors, and counter sales: 85, 40. 2) Mail subscriptions: 689, 565. C. Total paid circulation: 774, 605. D. Free distribution by mail, carrier, or other means (samples, complimentary, and other free copies): 125, 125. E. Total distribution (sum of C and D): 899, 730. F. Copies not distributed, 1) Office use, left over, unaccounted, spoiled after printing: 1759, 1940. 2) Returns from news agents: 0, 0. G. Total (sum of E, F1, and 2 — should equal net press run shown in A): 2658, 2670.

I certify that the statements made by me above are correct and complete.

JOHN R. WARD
Vice-President